CW01510184

PLOTINUS ON BEAUTY
(*ENNEADS* 1.6 AND 5.8.1–2)

WRITINGS FROM THE GRECO-ROMAN WORLD

General Editor
John T. Fitzgerald

Editorial Board
Christopher A. Baron
Andrew Cain
Margaret M. Mitchell
Teresa Morgan
Ilaria L. E. Ramelli
Clare K. Rothschild
David T. Runia
Karin Schlapbach
James C. VanderKam
L. Michael White

Number 44
Volume Editor
John Dillon

PLOTINUS ON BEAUTY
(*ENNEADS* 1.6 AND 5.8.1–2)

The Greek Text with Notes

Introduction and Commentary by
Andrew Smith

Copyright © 2019 by SBL Press

All rights reserved. No part of this work may be reproduced or transmitted in any form or by any means, electronic or mechanical, including photocopying and recording, or by means of any information storage or retrieval system, except as may be expressly permitted by the 1976 Copyright Act or in writing from the publisher. Requests for permission should be addressed in writing to the Rights and Permissions Office, SBL Press, 825 Houston Mill Road, Atlanta, GA 30329 USA.

Library of Congress Cataloging-in-Publication Data

Names: Plotinus, author. | Smith, Andrew, 1945– author, editor.
Title: Plotinus on beauty (Enneads 1.6 and 5.8.1-2) : the Greek text with notes / introduction and commentary by Andrew Smith.
Other titles: Enneads. Selections | Writings from the Greco-Roman world ; 44.
Description: Atlanta : SBL Press, 2019. | Series: Writings from the Greco-Roman world ; 44 | Includes bibliographical references.
Identifiers: LCCN 2019042407 | ISBN 9781628372489 (paperback) | ISBN 9780884143956 (hardcover) | ISBN 9780884143963 (ebook)
Subjects: LCSH: Plotinus. | Aesthetics—Early works to 1800.
Classification: LCC B693.A35 S65 2020 | DDC 186/.4—dc23
LC record available at https://lccn.loc.gov/2019042407

Printed on acid-free paper.

For Katie

Contents

Plotinus on Beauty

Abbreviations

Primary Sources

Ben.	Seneca, *De beneficiis*
Cels.	Origen, *Contra Celsum*
Civ.	Augustine, *De civitate Dei*
Comm. Arist.	Alexander of Aphrodisias, *Commentaria in Aristotelem Graeca*
Comm. somn. Scip.	Macrobius, *Commentarii in somnium Scipionis*
De an.	Aristotle, *De anima*
Descr.	Pausanius, *Graeciae descriptio*
Didask.	Alcinous, *Didaskalikos* (*The Handbook of Platonism*)
Ep.	Seneca, *Epistulae morales*
Eth. nic.	Aristotle, *Ethica nicomachea*
Gen. an.	Aristotle, *De generatione animalium*
Gorg.	Plato, *Gorgias*
Hipp. maj.	Plato, *Hippias major*
Hist. eccl.	Eusebius, *Historia ecclesiastica*
Imag.	Philostratus, *Imagines*
Leg.	Plato, *Leges*
Marc.	Porphyry, *Ad Marcellam*
Metam.	Ovid, *Metamorphoses*
Metaph.	Aristotle, *Metaphysica*
Od.	Homer, *Odyssey*
Or. Brut.	Cicero, *Orator ad M. Brutum*
Parm.	Plato, *Parmenides*
Part. an.	Aristotle, *De partibus animalium*
Phaed.	Plato, *Phaedo*
Phaedr.	Plato, *Phaedrus*
Phileb.	Plato, *Philebus*
Sent.	Porphyry, *Sententiae*

Soph.	Plato, *Sophista*
Symp.	Plato, *Symposium*
Theaet.	Plato, *Theaetetus*
Top.	Aristotle, *Topica*
Tusc.	Cicero, *Tusculanae disputationes*
Vit. Apoll.	Philostratus, *Vita Apollonii*
Vit. phil.	Diogenes Laertius, *Vitae philosophorum*
Vit. Plot.	Porphyry, *Vita Plotini*

Secondary Sources

BSGRT	Bibliotheca scriptorum Graecorum et Romanorum Teubneriana
DK	Diels, Hermann, and Walther Kranz. *Die Fragmente der Vorsokratiker.* 6th ed. 3 vols. RKLW 10. Zurich: Weidmann, 1954.
HS$_{1-5}$	Henry, Paul, and Hans-Rudolf Schwyer. *Plotini Opera.*
JAAC	*Journal of Aesthetics and Art Criticism*
LSJ	Liddell, Henry George, Robert Scott, Henry Stuart Jones. *A Greek-English Lexicon.* 9th ed. with revised supplement. Oxford: Clarendon, 1996.
NHC	Nag Hammadi codices
Smyth	Smyth, Herbert Weir. *Greek Grammar.* Revised by Gordon M. Messing. Cambridge: Harvard University Press, 1956.
SVF	Arnim, Hans Friedrich August von, ed. *Stoicorum Veterum Fragmenta.* Leipzig: Teubner, 1905–1924.

Introduction

Life of Plotinus

Plotinus (205–270 CE) was born in Egypt, a member of the extensive Greek community that had dominated Egyptian society since the conquests of Alexander the Great. He turned to philosophy at the age of twenty-eight and began to attend the philosophical schools of Alexandria, where he would have come into contact with the teaching of the main philosophical schools. But he seems to have been disappointed with what they had to offer and attached himself for eleven years to a certain Ammonius, about whom we unfortunately know very little but whose originality he admired.[1] In his desire to learn more about Indian philosophers (the Brahmans), he joined the disastrous military expedition of the emperor Gordian III against the Persians. After the defeat and death of the emperor (244 CE), he found his way to Rome, where he was later supported by the emperor Gallienus (253–268). It was here that he founded his own school that was accommodated in the house of a wealthy Roman woman. As in most ancient schools of philosophy, the number of students would have been relatively small. It attracted both professional philosophers, wealthy adherents (including Roman politicians and doctors), and interested members of the public, including some with gnostic leanings and possibly Christians, too. Plotinus was a gifted and inspiring teacher who preferred discussion to formal lecturing. This led to a reluctance to commit his ideas to writing, which he finally did only late in his career, possibly on the prompting of Porphyry, one of his most distinguished students. Plotinus's school was, like most ancient schools of philosophy, not primarily an academic institute but

---

1. See Porphyry, *Vit. Plot.* 3. The Christian Origen was also a student of Ammonius (see Eusebius, *Hist. eccl.* 6.19.6). This work formed Porphyry's introduction to his edition of the *Enneads* and is the main source of our information about the life of Plotinus.

rather a group of people seeking to live a particular mode of life under the direction of a master. Plotinus encouraged a modest and vegetarian life-style and evidently concerned himself with the well-being of the members of his circle; he was even entrusted with the care of young orphans whose education and welfare he personally promoted.

The Background to Plotinus's Thought

A convinced Platonist, Plotinus's life's work was devoted to interpreting and elucidating the thought of Plato. The treatise *On Beauty* was the first of a series of philosophical essays in which he dealt with the numerous issues encountered in this endeavor. Porphyry, who claimed the credit for encouraging him to set his thoughts down in writing, was primarily responsible for their final publication and ordering into six sets of nine treatises (hence the title *Enneads*) and adding titles to each piece. The *Enneads* may be considered the founding work of what we now call Neoplatonism, a term that was first used at the end of the eighteenth century in order to distinguish Plotinus and his followers from Plato himself. Plotinus, however, would have regarded himself simply as a Platonist, a follower of Plato, whose task was to interpret the works of Plato for his own students. Indeed, he rather modestly claims that he has nothing original to say, which is an enormous understatement. It is true that his treatment of Plato could be regarded as a plausible interpretation of the implications of the works of Plato, but Plotinus goes far beyond what we find in Plato in attempting to develop a single coherent account of the universe and humanity's place in it within the framework of Platonic ideas. Plotinus's account of the universe as a self-contained metaphysical system had been fully worked out by the time he began writing, but nowhere in the *Enneads* (except perhaps in 5.1) does he set this out in formal detail. He is more concerned to discuss the problems and issues arising from his system and to encourage his students (and us) to explore them critically. In fact, his written style is such as to transport us into the cut and thrust of philosophical debate within his own seminars. The treatise *On Beauty* is one of the most accessible and influential of his treatises, and although in no sense composed as a formal introduction to his thought, it nevertheless provides, in a short compass, a stimulating entrée to the many facets of his philosophical activity.

We need to be aware, then, of the Platonic ideas that he is trying to explicate and develop. However, despite his overwhelming importance, Plato is for Plotinus no isolated figure but rather one who is central in the development of Greek philosophy as a whole. For example, the Presocratic philosophers are often cited by Plotinus as dimly forestalling Platonic ideas. Moreover, Plato, he implies, left many concepts unfinished or needing further explanation or development. In this sense even the Platonic criticisms of Aristotle help to elucidate his thought, a procedure that led Porphyry to remark on the profound influence of Aristotle's metaphysics on Plotinus. The Hellenistic philosophical movements, particularly the Stoics, also contributed to his task of elucidating Plato, not least in presenting the notion of a systematic presentation of the universe and humanity's place within it as an ethical and spiritual agent. Of course, Plato's own school, the Academy and its various successors,[2] provided a constantly evolving Platonic interpretation on which Plotinus could also draw for ideas and inspiration. Not only the original works of Plato but the many commentaries on his dialogues and on the works of Aristotle produced in the philosophical schools of the early empire up to his own time were read in his seminars and often provided the starting point for discussion. Unfortunately, much of the material available to Plotinus and his students is lost to us, and the complex development of philosophy in the early imperial period is only imperfectly understood. It would be a mistake to think that Plotinus's rich reinterpretation of Plato emerged purely from a reading of the Platonic texts. Rather, it is a development of the diverse and changing perspectives and debates of preceding centuries. But Plotinus's original genius is all the greater for his ability to come to grips with the most challenging contemporary metaphysical issues and rise above them with often novel and penetrating insights.

General Outline of Plotinus's Philosophical System

Before beginning to read the treatise *On Beauty*, it will be helpful to have the sort of general knowledge of his system as a whole that his own students would already have had. While much of Plotinus's metaphysical structure is recognizably an interpretation of Plato, it is an interpretation that is not always immediately obvious just because it is filtered through several centuries of developing Platonic thought, itself already overlaid with important concepts drawn from other schools. It is, nevertheless,

---

2. The "official" Academy, located in Athens, was in Plotinus's time led by Longinus, one of whose pupils was Porphyry, who later sent his previous master copies of Plotinus's treatises.

useful as a starting point to see how Plotinus attempts to bring coherence to what he believed to be a comprehensive worldview expressed in
the Platonic dialogues. The Platonic Forms are central. They become for
him an intelligible universe (κόσμος νοητός) that is the source and model
of the physical universe. But aware of Aristotle's criticism of the Platonic
Forms as lifeless causes, he takes on board Aristotle's concept of god as a
self-thinker to enable him to identify this intelligible universe as a divine
Intellect that thinks itself as the Forms or Intelligibles. The doctrine of
the Forms as the thoughts of god had already entered Platonism, but not
as the rigorously argued identity that Plotinus proposed. Moreover, the
Intelligibles, since they are identical with Intellect, are themselves actively
intellectual; they are intellects. Thus Plato's world of Forms has become a
complex and dynamic intelligible universe in which unity and plurality,
stability and activity are reconciled.

Now although the divine Intellect is one, it also embraces plurality
both because its thoughts, the Intelligibles, are many and because it may
itself be analyzed into thinker and thought. Its unity demands a further
principle that is the cause of its unity. This principle, which is the cause
of all unity and being but does not possess unity or being in itself, Plotinus calls the One, an interpretation of the Idea of the Good in Plato's
Republic that is "beyond being" and that may be seen as the simple (hence
"one") source of all reality. We thus have the first two of what subsequently
became known as the three hypostases: the One and Intellect. The third is
Soul, which acts as an intermediary between the transcendent and physical universes, or rather is the immediate cause of this physical universe.
This last hypostasis takes on all the functions of transmitting form and life,
which may be found in Plato, although Plato himself does not always make
such a clear distinction between soul and intellect. Thus the One is the
ultimate source of all, including this universe, which is then prefigured in
Intellect and transmitted through Soul to become manifest as our physical
universe. Matter, which receives imperfectly this expression, is conceived
not as an independently existing counterprinciple, a dangerously dualist
notion, but is in a sense itself a product of the One, a kind of nonbeing
that, while being nothing specific in itself, nevertheless is not simply not
there.

This procession from an ultimate principle is balanced by a return
movement at each level of reality, which fully constitutes itself only when
it turns back in contemplation of its producer. So the whole of reality is
a dynamic movement from stability (μονή) to procession (πρόοδος) and

return (ἐπιστροφή), except for matter, which has no life of its own to make this return; it is inert. This movement of return, which may be traced back to the force of ἔρως in Plato or Aristotle's final cause, is characterized by Plotinus as a cognitive activity, a form of contemplation, weaker at each successive level, from Intellect through discursive reasoning to the merest image of rational order as expressed in the objects of the physical universe.

The human individual mirrors this structure to which we are all related at each level, for each of us has a body, a soul, an intellect, and even something within us that relates to the One. While it is the nature of soul to give life to body, the higher aspect of our soul also has aspirations toward intellect, the true self, and even beyond. This urge to return corresponds to the cosmic movement of return. But the tension between soul's natural duty to body and its origins in the intelligible can be, for the individual, a source of fracture and alienation in which the soul becomes overinvolved and overwhelmed by the body and so estranged from its true self. Plotinus encourages us to make the return or ascent, but at the same time he attempts to resolve the conflict of duties by reconciling the twofold nature of soul as life-giving and contemplative. What, then, is a person's function within this world order? Just as for Plato, this is not merely a matter of how a human can know (epistemology) but also of how a human acts (ethics). In the eyes of most ancient philosophers epistemology and ethics, rational and spiritual progress, are intimately connected. For Plotinus, "doing philosophy" also means acting morally with spiritual integrity. Then just what is most essential in humans? We are endowed not only with a body but with a soul, akin to the world Soul, and with an intellect, which is akin to the universal Intellect. Discursive thinking is the work of the soul, but above this we have a faculty of intuitive thought that is the ultimate source of our discursive thinking, a distinction that Plotinus found in Plato's two levels of cognition: discursive thinking (διάνοια) and true knowledge (ἐπιστήμη). The challenge is to activate within us these various faculties that we possess but do not always use, to empower the "I" or self at each level. We begin by moving from merely bodily concerns to the cultivation of virtue and rational thought. From rational thought we progress to a direct encounter with ideas by identifying ourselves with our intellect. And just as our intellect can be one with the universal Intellect, so also there is something within us which can be united with the One itself. It is in this final stage that we may speak of a mystical experience, but a mysticism that is the culmination of a philosophical rather than religious procedure. Nor does this imply a flight from the everyday world, for each level attained informs and enriches the activities of the lower self. Porphyry recounts Plotinus's concern for those around him, his care of orphans entrusted to him, and his calling on Porphyry in his lodgings when he was suffering from depression. In Porphyry's words, "He was present to himself and others at the same time" (*Vit. Plot.* 8.19); that is, he could reconcile the life of contemplation and of action.

Let us now turn more closely to the treatise *On Beauty,* to point out those features that illustrate his philosophical style, as well as the numerous, not always obvious, references to his central philosophical concepts. For within its few pages one can recognize many of the features of Plotinus's philosophical method, and as he develops his theme we catch glimpses of the essential metaphysical ideas that underlie his inquiry.

The treatise begins with an academic discussion and criticism of current theories of beauty. The search for an adequate concept of what beauty is and what causes beauty very quickly leads us away from physically based explanations to a transcendent cause. However, this transcendent cause can only be reached by a process that is at once rigorously rational but at the same time deeply personal, by looking into oneself and rediscovering true beauty through the different levels of the self. No one can do this for us; we must achieve it ourselves. It is in this dual spirit that the treatise reaches is climax. It will be found that many of his treatises follow this pattern of philosophical discourse leading to personal discovery through exhortation. In fact, the very core of Plotinus's epistemology is the claim that true knowledge occurs only when the knower becomes identical with the object of knowledge, that is, in a direct and personal encounter. It is Plotinus's response to the skeptics' claim that we can know an object only as external to ourselves and that therefore we possess only an image of it and not the object itself (5.5.1–2). True knowledge is, then, possible only when we "become" the object of knowledge, an idea expressed in 1.6.9,15, "if you have become this" (εἰ γέγονας τοῦτο), where the transition to intellect marks the radical distinction that Plotinus draws between soul and intellect.

Despite its title, this treatise is not primarily a discourse on aesthetics but rather an exhortation to lead the philosophical life, which takes its starting point from an innate urge to rediscover, from the expressions of beauty in the universe, the transcendent beauty that is its cause and that will be found to lie in the depths of our own soul and intellect, which is, in its turn, at one with the universal Intellect. This is the journey advocated by Diotima in Plato's *Symposium* and that fulfills the Platonic goal of life "to become like god" (*Theaet.* 176b1). And it is the *Symposium* and

Phaedrus that also provide the close link between love and beauty that Plotinus exploits. It first emerges in chapter 4 as an expression of that power of attraction that is exercised by beauty, as already explained in the previous two chapters. The response of love and desire is, for Plotinus, one of the most basic dynamic forces of the universe, for it is both the intrinsic power of all things to desire the Good as they turn to contemplate their causes (ἐπιστροφή, cf. 1.6.7,2 [οὗ ὀρέγεται πᾶσα ψυχή] and 10–11 [πρὸς αὐτὸ βλέπει...]), thus securing their own perfection and also, in the case of the individual, the source of our ability to find our real selves by returning to our originative cause and so assimilating ourselves to god. The opening chapter of the treatise *On Love* (3.5[50]) has ideas very similar to those in 1.6, particularly in the description of the soul's initial response to beauty and ugliness in 1.6.2 and 3.

> Then everyone, of course, realizes that the affection for which we say love is responsible occurs in souls that desire to be closely bound with beauty of some kind and that this desire comes in one form from the self-controlled who have discovered their affinity with beauty itself, but in another form also seeks to find its culmination in the performance of some base person. Where each takes its rise is a proper topic to pursue in a philosophical way in what follows. If one were to posit as its origin the longing for beauty itself which is already present in human souls, their recognition of it, kinship with it, and subrational awareness of their affinity with it, one would, I think, hit on the truth about its cause. (3.5[50].1,10–19)

The impetus toward beauty and the Good is already built into our nature, as an urge that is almost unconsciously present, although, Plotinus recognizes, it can be employed to perverse ends. He then goes on in this passage to speak of our instinctive rejection of what is ugly, an idea similarly found in 1.6.

A further feature of beauty that marks it as an important concept is its being more than simply one Form among others at the level of Intellect. In fact, we might argue that it is not a Form at all, for it is a feature of the Intelligible World in its entirety and, in a sense, is identical with the Intelligible World. Another section from the same chapter describes it as akin to eternity, which is not a Form but an essential property of Being:

> And the man whose love of beauty is pure will love beauty alone whether he has recalled the archetype or not, while the man whose love is mixed

with another appetite, for "being immortal as far as is possible for a mortal,"[3] seeks what is beautiful in the "everlasting"[4] and eternal, and as he proceeds according to nature he sows and begets in beauty, the sowing being to perpetuate himself, and it is done in beauty because of the kinship of beauty and eternity. For eternity is certainly akin to beauty, and the eternal nature[5] is the first to be beautiful, and all that proceeds from it is beautiful. (3.5.1,37–46)

Beauty thus joins Eternity in the company of the five genera of Being, Sameness, Difference, Movement, and Rest that Plotinus took from Plato's *Sophist* as defining his Intelligible World.

Beauty and Aesthetic Theory in 1.6 and 5.8

I have included the first two chapters of 5.8 to complement what 1.6. has to say about beauty in this world. Both endorse and supplement the earlier discussion, but their context and purpose are profoundly different: 1.6 is concerned with how the individual soul can return to its origins and its original beauty through the rediscovery of the successively higher levels of beauty that it may be trained to encounter and recognize; the emphasis of 5.8. lies rather on the universal and cosmic dimension of beauty. Of course 5.8 is, as are most treatises of Plotinus, concerned with the individual soul—witness, for example, the similarity of ideas with 1.6 when he suggests (5.8.9,11–12) that we must hone the beauty in ourselves as a prerequisite for finding the beauty of others or of the intelligible universe, as well as the undoubtedly very personal and almost mystical experience of his vision of an intelligible world of interpenetrating Forms (5.8.4,10–11).

Plotinus begins with the argument that physical beauty must come from something outside and above the matter in which it is expressed. In the case of artistic beauty (e.g., a statue), one can point to the form in the artist's mind, in that of natural beauty (e.g., a stone) to the form that provides beauty to the underlying matter. These forms, which are higher than the immanent form that they bring to matter, are more beautiful than their instantiation in the physical world.

---

3. Plato, *Symp.* 206e8
4. Plato, *Symp.* 206e8.
5. I.e., Intellect.

Chapter 2 of 5.8 concludes with the call to look beyond the mere physical manifestations of beauty to the form within an object, then yet further, away from all externals, to beauty that has no physical manifestation, such as the goodness within someone who might even have an ugly appearance. But to attain this we must prepare ourselves (make ourselves beautiful).

This preparation leads us (5.8.3) beyond discursive reason to encounter the intelligible world, the source of beauty, through the direct vision of our intellect. What this sort of cognition involves and how we can attain it provides the subject matter of the rest of the treatise.

Plato and Plotinus on Art as Imitation

Although Plotinus never proposes a theory of art in itself and the discussions of art in 1.6 and 5.8 are incidental to the main purpose of the treatises, it is nevertheless possible to abstract from them some important elements of artistic theory. The first two chapters of 5.8 complement Plotinus's discussion of physical beauty in 1.6. Particularly significant is their extensive comparison of artistic and natural beauty; Plotinus here also introduces art and the role of the artist, whereas art, as opposed to beauty, is only implied in 1.6. In 5.8 he stresses the nature of art as imitative, not, however, of any physical object, as in Plato's *Republic*, but of the ideal form.[6] In this context he notes that the artist can even improve on nature (5.8.1,36–37). In these respects Plotinus's view of art does not follow Plato's analysis of art in the *Republic* (book 10, 596a–599b), where it is criticized as being imitative of physical objects and standing at a third remove from the ideal Form behind the material object represented by the artist. Plotinus's theory echoes rather the metaphysics of the *Symposium*, where beauty is traced back to its transcendent cause, and the status of art (poetry) in the *Phaedrus*, where it is an expression of divine inspiration. Presumably Plotinus would not see a contradiction here but would suppose that in the *Republic* Plato is considering a different context (politics/education) and, perhaps also, a different kind of art, one on a lower level. Hence possibly his refusal to have his portrait painted (Porphyry, *Vit. Plot.* 1), since this really would be at a third remove, an imitation of a particular

---

6. See also 5.9[5].5,40–41, referring to Plato's "true bed," i.e. the transcendent as opposed to the immanent form of bed in the physical object.

physical reality. The sort of art that Plotinus perhaps has in mind in 5.8 is the kind of idealistic sculpture represented by Phidias's statue of Zeus at Olympia, mentioned at the end of the first chapter. The ground seems already to have been prepared for such an "idealizing" trend in interpreting Plato. It appears already in Cicero (*Or. Brut.* 2.8–3.9) and in Seneca (*Ep.* 65.8), in the latter as a combination of Stoic, Platonic, and Aristotelian doctrines that probably goes back to Antiochus, a Stoicizing Platonist of the first century BCE. An interesting similarity of approach may also be found in the discussion by Dio of Prusa, an orator and cynic of the second century CE, of Phidias's Zeus in his *Olympian Oration* (*Or.* 12), where he makes Phidias defend his representation of the god in human form and show that it does not diminish his real stature. All of this suggests that Plotinus was not out of touch with contemporary popular theories of art and, far from criticizing Plato, would have thought that he was correctly interpreting Plato's "real intent" against possible misinterpretation (see also the commentary on 5.8.1,32–40.).

Another reason, too, for Plotinus's positive evaluation of artistic beauty may lie in his exploration of the way in which we make the ascent to the intelligible world. It is significant that Plotinus begins the treatise 5.8 with an analysis of artistic rather than natural beauty. This stress on artistic beauty and its explanation in terms of form and apprehension of form is fueled by his own optimistic view of the human ability to reach the level of Intellect and its beauty, particularly since for him the individual intellect then becomes one with the universal Intellect. The idea that artists have within them an idea of beauty that derives directly from the intelligible world in fact coincides with his theory that each one of us has access to Intellect through our own intellects. It is the exploitation of this theme that forms the central dynamic of the treatise, with its stress on our ability to "see" and be one with the intelligible world and its beauty.

The combination of ideas from 5.8 and 1.6, transmitted partly through Marsilio Ficino, has had a profound influence on artistic theory from the time of the Renaissance and remains still relevant to modern debate, and this influence has ensured in no small measure the popularity of the treatise *On Beauty*. It must, however, be constantly borne in mind that, although Plotinus invested much profound thought into the nature of beauty and art, this was for him a side issue and an almost incidental consequence of his primary consideration, which was to explain the relationship of this world to its transcendent archetype and indicate the way in which we might return to our true selves and "become like god."

Beauty as Symmetry

The idea that symmetry is an important aspect of beauty was fairly commonplace in Greek thought. It appears in Plato and Aristotle[7] but was particularly espoused by the Stoics. In *Phileb.* 64e7–8, Plato includes symmetry as a component of the Good along with Beauty. In the *Timaeus*, right proportions are regarded as important for the universe (31c) and for the equilibrium of body and soul (87c). Finally, in *Soph.* 235e6–7, symmetry (with color) is seen as an important element in art.[8] The conjunction of symmetry and color is found as Stoic teaching in Cicero's *Tusculan Disputations*, in which the health of soul is compared with beauty of the body:

> And as in the body a certain symmetrical shape of the limbs combined with a certain charm of coloring is described as beauty, so in the soul the name of beauty is given to an equipoise and consistency of beliefs and judgments, following upon virtue or comprising the true essence of virtue.[9] (*Tusc.* 4.31)

It is taken up again by Augustine (*Civ.* 22.19).

Plotinus recognizes the widespread nature of the theory when he says that it was held "by all," but it should be noted that he immediately qualifies this remark (παρὰ πάντων, ὡς εἰπεῖν), since he is aware that Plato at least did not make it in any sense an exclusive or essential factor. So, for example, in the *Philebus* pleasure and beauty are found in simple noncomposites:

> [True pleasures are] those that attach to colors that we call beautiful, to figures, to most odours, to sounds … things like that, I maintain, are

---

7. For Aristotle, see *Top.* 3, 116b21: "The beauty of melodies is a kind of symmetry"; and *Metaph.* 1078a36: "The chief forms of beauty are order, symmetry, and definiteness."

8. It should, however, be noted that the status of art in this passage is relatively low and that the idea is introduced in order to contrast with what Plato regards as an even more inferior form of art that permits the contravention of the natural laws of proportion.

9. Et ut corporis est quaedam apta figura membrorum cum coloris quadam suavitate eaque dicitur pulchritudo, sic in animo opinionum iudiciorumque aequabilitas et constantia cum firmitate quadam et stabilitate virtutem subsequens aut virtutis vim ipsam continens pulchritudo vocatur (cf. SVF 3.278–79).

beautiful not, like most things, in a relative sense; they are always beautiful in their very nature, and they carry pleasures peculiar to themselves
… and there are colors too which have this characteristic … audible
sounds which are smooth and clear, and deliver a single series of pure
notes, are beautiful and not relative to something else, but in themselves.
(51b3–d8 [Hackforth])

Despite, however, the emphasis in this treatise on the Platonic notion of a
transcendent cause of beauty, we should be clear that Plotinus is not ruling
out altogether the contribution of symmetry to beauty. So, for example, in
6.7.22, in drawing an analogy between the experience of intellectual and
physical beauty, he clearly suggests that symmetry constitutes a certain
element of beauty in physical objects,[10] and in 2.9.16,41–42 symmetry is
recognized as contributing to the beauty of the physical universe, though
in both cases this is rather as effect than as cause. But it remains for Plotinus
inadmissible as an explanation of the cause of beauty because it runs coun-
ter to his metaphysical concept of the universe as a cosmic unity whose
wholeness and unity is dependent on and is an expression of a transcendent intelligible cause. It is for this reason that he pays so much attention to
disproving the cogency of the theory of symmetry. His arguments concern
not only physical beauty but also the incorporeal beauty of the activities of
soul. Against the former he claims that symmetry does not account for the
beauty of things that are singular and without parts, although it is worth
noting that the beauty of the simple also, and more significantly, applies to
the intelligible world, which, strictly speaking, is a unity and without parts.
Against the latter he argues that symmetry cannot account for the beauty
of ideas and virtue, values that are ultimately of more interest to him than
physical beauty. But his arguments are not entirely cogent and convincing
(see Anton 1964). Some of the weak points include his failure to analyze
further the possibly different meanings of simplicity in the examples he
gives (gold, lightning, a musical note) or the equation of symmetry and
conformity in his analysis of propositions. Yet a failure to discount the
case for symmetry does not disprove and need not impair the value of

---

10. See 6.7.22,24–29, where he says that "beauty is what illuminates good proportions rather than the good proportions themselves" and then goes on to say that "there
is more light of beauty on a living face, but only a trace of it on a dead one," thus implying that there is some beauty, if only a trace (ἴχνος), on a dead person's face.

Plotinus's own preferred explanation of the cause of beauty, which could be accepted as a more comprehensive and explanatory theory.

The Value of Physical Beauty

But is physical beauty merely a means to an end with no intrinsic value of its own and so to be ignored or even rejected by philosophers who have assimilated themselves to the divine? There are a number of indications that Plotinus would not agree with such a view. It is not merely a ladder to be cast away after use; 3.5.1 is particularly explicit about this. He has already distinguished three different kinds of love of beauty in the first half of the chapter, part of which is cited above: love of incorporeal beauty, heterosexual love, and homosexual love, which he condemns. When he returns to the topic, he makes it clear that, although the first kind differs from the second in that it does not find physical love and beauty sufficient, he does, nevertheless, still value it.

> But, to return to the point, those who love beautiful bodies, but not[11] for sexual reasons, love them because they are beautiful and there are also those who have the love which is called[12] mixed, for women in order to perpetuate themselves, but if it is love for other than women they are making a mistake. The first group are better, but both the first and the second are morally sound. But while the latter reverence earthly beauty too and find it sufficient, the former reverence beauty in the other realm insofar as they have recalled it and yet do not disdain beauty here, given that it can be a fulfilment of beauty there and its playful expression. These then are concerned with beauty without ugliness, but there are those others who fall into ugliness even though it is on account of beauty. For the desire of good often involves the fall into evil. (3.5.1,55–65)

Another important, and more metaphysical, point comes out in the passage from 6.7.22,29–34, which was mentioned above in speaking of symmetry:

> And are not the more lifelike [ζωτικώτερα] statues the more beautiful ones, even if the others are better proportioned? And is not an uglier living human more beautiful than the beautiful human in a statue? Yes,

11. Negative μή added with Ficino (1433–1499), Flamand, and Kalligas.
12. See Plato, *Leg.* 837b.

because the living [ζῶν] is more desirable, and this is because it has soul, and this is because it has more the form of good, and this means that it is somehow colored by the light of the Good.

Plotinus here notes that a statue that is more lifelike is more attractive; so also a living human who is ugly is more beautiful than the most handsome statue. The key here is *life*, and the presence of life is due to the presence and activity of soul, which communicates and irradiates the Good throughout the universe.[13] The implication is that the living human has a greater soul presence than a beautiful statue. In this sense Socrates is beautiful though visually ugly in the conventional sense. It is striking that Plotinus here seems to discount the ugliness of the face, an ugliness that is presumably also due to the absence of form. But Socrates's beauty still remains a physical beauty, so that we must presume that the beauty of life bestowed on the face by the soul must somehow override the other failings. We may also ask whether the beauty of the living face is quantitative, in the sense that the living face manifests the presence of those form/soul powers such as movement that are not present in the statue, or qualitative, in that the living face manifests, for example, the inner qualities of the person (see Porphyry's account of how Plotinus could read character from a person's external appearance, *Vit. Plot.* 11).

In 5.8.2,27–28 Plotinus offers some further reflections on physical beauty. He argues that physical beauty is perceived as immanent form along with the externally expressed attributes such as size as they are taken in through the eyes: "But the size is drawn in along with it, since it has become not large in bulk but 'large' in form" (συνεφέλκεται δὲ καὶ τὸ μέγεθος οὐ μέγα ἐν ὄγκῳ, ἀλλ᾽ εἴδει γενόμενον μέγα). This indicates that the object as perceived, although entirely constituted of forms, is perceived *as an object with physical properties* and is thus different from the ideal, which is without such manifested physical properties. When Plotinus goes on in this passage to complain that we normally observe only the external manifestations of beauty without understanding the causal working of the immanent form in things, he seems to be advocating that we look only at the inner form and discount its physical expression:

---

13. Note, too, the introduction of the notion of ζωή in 1.6.7,11.

But the beauty also in studies and ways of life and generally in souls makes clear that what is pursued is something else and that beauty does not lie in magnitude: it is truly a greater beauty than that when you see moral sense in someone and delight in it, not looking at his face—which might be ugly—but putting aside all shape and pursuing his inner beauty. (5.8.2,37–41)

But taken in the light of the previous lines, the phrase "not looking at his face" should indicate not that we should ignore physical presence altogether but should rather ignore the deficiencies of purely external beauty and see the manifestations of inner beauty. From this we then progress to viewing the internal beauty alone when the immanent form is compared with the form of beauty within our own souls.

We must finally take into account the fact that Plotinus fully recognizes that we are embodied human beings and in this way always attached to and indeed dependent on the physical environment in which we live. Although the ultimate goal is complete freedom from the body and unity with Intellect and the One, Plotinus does not himself place any great weight on a purely physical disengagement, that is, a physical separation of soul and body after death. This is the import of a vivid comparison of the series of our embodied lives with the activities of an actor who enters the stage wearing different masks, or even in different plays, while remaining the same actor (3.2.15,24–25). Thus the same person remains behind the changes of masks or throughout a series of reincarnations. The implication of this is that we never lose the link with a physical body and that our inner life may be promoted within the context of our physical existence. Thus our physical environment remains very much part of what we are: a complex being living at different levels. To this extent the beauty of the physical universe still remains relevant to us.

The Influence of Plotinus's Theory of Beauty

Marsilio Ficino (1433–1499) can claim to have been the main source of Plotinian ideas about beauty that influenced numerous Renaissance thinkers and artists.[14] We should not, however, ignore Augustine's influence as a source both for the Western tradition in general and for Ficino himself. Although it still remains unclear whether Augustine had direct

---

14. For the influence of Plotinus on Ficino's theory of beauty, see Beierwaltes 1980.

access to the *Enneads* either in Greek or in a Latin translation, it is possible to detect the influence of 1.6 in particular. He cites it loosely in *City of God* (*Civ.* 9.17), where he mentions the name of Plotinus and combines phrases from 1.6.8,16 and 21–22. The description of the vision of God in *Civ.* 10.16 recalls 1.6.7, and at one point Augustine seems to be referring directly to 1.6.7,33–34.[15]

Ficino both translated and commented on the *Enneads* as well as develop Plotinus's ideas on art as fundamental topics in his other works (e.g., *De Amore, Theologia Platonica*). Basic was the intimate connection, as in Plato and Plotinus, between Goodness and Beauty, morality and artistic creation. Among the most influential ideas that he developed from Plotinus is the notion that the divine is the cause of beauty: God as light and source of beauty: "concludamus pulchritudinem esse gratiam quamdam vivacem et spiritalem, dei radio illustrante … que per rationem, visum, auditum animos nostros movet atque delectat, delectando rapit, rapiendo ardenti inflammat amore" (*De Amore* 5.6,190). Ficino also promoted the Plotinian interpretation of Plato that the artist has direct access to the forms, for the artist "imitates" the forms in the strong and positive sense of re-expressing or producing them at another level of reality and even perfecting them ("materias illas excellentiores reddat," *Theologia Platonica* 13.3). Fundamental, too, for Ficino's artistic theory is the concept of *amor*, the innate human capacity to strive toward the divine and thus to link the physical with the intelligible and transcendent universe. Perhaps one of the most striking features of Ficino's Neoplatonism was his interpretation of the three Graces, which seems to lie behind the Primavera of Botticelli (1445–1510). For Ficino the Graces were a symbol of the fundamental dynamic of Neoplatonic metaphysics (μονή πρόοδος ἐπιστροφή), the cyclical movement of creation and return: *creare—rapere—perficere*.[16]

To take just one practicing artist, some of these ideas may be found in the poetry of Michelangelo (1474–1564), although it is difficult to be certain whether he was influenced directly or indirectly by Ficino:

Ravished by all that to the eyes is fair,
Yet hungry for the joys that truly bless,

---

15. For the influence of Plotinus on Augustine, see Smith 2016.

16. Cf. Wind 1968, 37–38, 120–21. But Wind rightly notes (38 n. 9) that Ficino adjusts the first item of the triad by emphasizing the activity of creation rather than stability.

My soul can find no stair
To mount to heaven, save earth's loveliness.
For from the stars above
Descends a glorious light
That lifts our longing to their highest height
And bears the name of love.
Nor is there aught can move
A gentle heart, or purge or make it wise,
But beauty and the starlight of her eyes.[17]

Plotinus's Greek

Plotinus' Greek has the notorious reputation for being difficult and obscure. Even in antiquity his brevity was noted by Macrobius,[18] and Porphyry, in his introduction to his edition of the *Enneads*, is somewhat critical of Plotinus's fluency in exposition and of his mistakes in diction and spelling (Porphyry, *Vit. Plot.* 13), as well as his practice of never rereading and correcting what he had written. We should also bear in mind that Plotinus much preferred oral discussion to formal lecturing and did not, in fact, commit his ideas to written form until quite late in his career (Porphyry, *Vit. Plot.* 4,5). His style of composition often reflects the lively debate of a philosophical seminar rather than a formal presentation of his views. Objections, counterobjections and modifications to his arguments follow in often bewildering succession. But a patient and careful reading reveals the flexibility, originality, and openness of his philosophizing, characteristics that were clearly recognized by his own contemporaries.[19] He evidently composed in a continuous manner without rereading or revising what he had already written. But despite these many obstacles, we should always be alert to the cogent construction of his arguments aided by the careful positioning of particles.

Readers of Plotinus's Greek may usefully be prepared for some of the difficulties they will encounter.

---

17. Trans. George Santayana.

18. Macrobius, *Comm. somn. Scip.* 2.12.7: "Plotinus magis quam quisquam verborum parcus." Longinus may be thinking of the same trait when he speaks of the πυκνότης (denseness) of his ideas (Porphyry, *Vit. Plot.* 19,38).

19. E.g., Porphyry (*Vit. Plot.* 13,2) and Longinus (*Vit. Plot.* 19,37–41) .

Macrobius's remark about his brevity (*verborum parcus*) may be illustrated by a number of features:

- frequent omission of the verb "to be" (e.g., 1.6.1,8; 1.6.2,13–15)
- omission of μέν before a contrasting δέ (1.6.8,13) or of a first negative before a following οὐδε, or similarly one εἴτε where there should be two
- referent of a pronoun is often unclear and must be inferred from the sense (e.g., 1.6.3,1: αὐτό is τὸ κάλλος)
- accumulation of participles (1.6.9,22–24), often depending on each other (5.8.2,4–6) or in asyndeton
- sentences without predicate
- accusative and infinitive with no finite verb, suggesting the omission of a verb of saying or the like; editors have sometimes inserted δεῖ
- a participle instead of a finite verb

Unexpected changes and inconsistencies of syntax:

- anacolouthon (1.6.1,2: τε … ἔστι δὲ καί)
- gnomic aorist used together with the present (1.6.9,9: ἀφαιρεῖ … ἀπέξεσε)
- change between neuter and masculine referring to the same thing (1.6.7,10–11: πρὸς αὐτὸ βλέπει … ζωῆς γὰρ αἴτιος)
- singular to plural change (1.6.8,6–7: ἰδόντα … γνόντας)
- genitive absolute where not necessary

Usages commonly found in philosophical texts:

- use of a neuter adjective with a masculine or feminine noun (1.6.6,17 and 19)
- particle ἤ (to be distinguished from ἤ meaning "or") used often, as in Aristotle, for the correction of a previous assertion or the introduction of a further possibility

Other peculiarities:

- ambiguity of syntax (1.6,1,30)
- article used with predicate
- attribute in predicative position
- article with interrogative pronoun
- omission of ἄν in potential construction
- μή used where one would expect οὐ

- τε often where there is no second τε or καί
- A serious problem arises from Plotinus's apparent use of the oblique forms of αὐτός as a reflexive, that is, without the rough breathing. Interpreters have usually tried to follow the consensus of the manuscripts, but their compilers were not infallible. Each case must be considered on its merits within the philosophical context.

However, at times Plotinus's style rises to grandeur of expression as can be seen in the concluding chapters of the treatise *On Beauty*, for example, the long, laboring sentence at 1.6.9.8–15 that expresses well the effort required to lead the philosophical life. Here he also makes use of rhetorical devices (chiasmus, tricola, and repetition). Chiasmus is found elsewhere (1.6.1,39–40), and careful positioning of words is used for emphasis (e.g., 1.6.3,1). An earnest philosophical style of exhortation is frequently achieved, for example, by changing the address from the third- to the more personal second-person singular (1.6.5,6–7; 8,23; 9,5). His range of expression is also enriched with the often-colorful vocabulary of Plato. In these ways Plotinus combines the relentless and often dry logic of Aristotle with the poetic beauty of Plato's prose.

The Greek Text with Notes

1.6. *On Beauty*

Chapter 1

Although the treatise begins with a discussion of physical beauty, it is immediately made clear that beauty is found beyond this. Moreover, the search for beauty is more than a purely intellectual enquiry, since beauty stirs and moves us (κινεῖ ... ἐπιστρέφει ... ἕλκει ... εὐφραίνεσθαι ... ποιεῖ, 6,17–19), which introduces the context of moral and spiritual progress from Plato, *Symp.* 210a–212a. Plotinus then (*Enn.* 1.6–16) poses a number of questions that are answered in the course of the treatise:

1. Is there beauty beyond the virtues? (1.6): answered in 6,26–32 with the mention of beauty at the level of Intellect and the One.
2. What causes our perception of physical beauty? (1.7–8): answered in chapters 2 and 3 by introducing the idea of embodied form.
3. How can incorporeals (ὅσα ψυχῆς ἔχεται) be beautiful? (1.9): answered in chapters 4 and 5 with the identification of beauty with being.
4. To the related set of questions (Is there one cause of beauty or one for bodies and another for incorporeals? What is the cause of beauty in bodies? [1.10–16]), the complex response, that the cause is Form at different levels, emerges gradually as the analysis of the treatise unfolds.

The chapter concludes (6,20–54) with a critique of the popular and widespread theory that closely connects symmetry and beauty. Although the chapter is critical of this idea, it is not entirely rejected but seen as inadequate, for even if symmetry may sometimes be a component of beauty, it is an effect rather than a cause (see introduction above, pp. 11–13).

1.6. ΠΕΡΙ ΤΟΥ ΚΑΛΟΥ

1. Τὸ καλὸν ἔστι μὲν ἐν ὄψει πλεῖστον, ἔστι δ' ἐν ἀκοαῖς κατά τε λόγων συνθέσεις, ἔστι δὲ καὶ ἐν μουσικῇ καὶ
ἁπάσῃ· καὶ γὰρ μέλη καὶ ῥυθμοί εἰσι καλοί· ἔστι δὲ καὶ
προιοῦσι πρὸς τὸ ἄνω ἀπὸ τῆς αἰσθήσεως καὶ ἐπιτηδεύματα καλὰ καὶ πράξεις καὶ ἕξεις καὶ ἐπιστῆμαί τε καὶ τὸ   5

1,1. ὄψει … ἀκοαῖς. The emphasis on beauty in sight and hearing may
be a reminiscence of Plato, *Hipp. maj.* 297e–298a. Socrates then goes on
(298b2) to mention ἐπιτηδεύματα and νόμοι.

1,2. We would expect τε to be picked up by καί rather than ἔστιν δὲ καὶ.
This sort of anacolouthon suggests strongly the live seminar nature of Plotinus's style of composition, as if he is creatively thinking as he writes. Here
he begins by clearly distinguishing sight and hearing, but when he comes
to a further division of hearing between words and music, having mentioned words he seems to have realized that music is a more complicated
category. Hence the reemphasis with the repeated ἔστι. I also prefer to
keep the second καί (καὶ ἁπάσῃ), which some editors (Kirkhoff, Theiler)
have found awkwardly redundant and deleted. It serves to emphasize the
complex nature of music ("indeed in all aspects of music"), which Plotinus
goes on to explain in the following sentence, which instances melody and
rhythm.

1,3. A similar pair of components of music, designated as "all music," is
found in *Enn.* 5.9.11,9: rhythm and harmony (ἁρμονία), the latter perhaps
corresponding to "melody."

καὶ προιοῦσι. καὶ emphasizes that he is now moving from physical sensations of beauty to those that are incorporeal. "Those who rise above from
the physical also experience beauty...."

1,4–5. ἐπιτηδεύματα and ἐπιστῆμαι are found in *Symp.* 210c6. Plotinus's
list becomes progressively less physical and represents an ascending and
hierarchical scale: ἐπιτηδεύματα, occupations and modes of conducting
oneself; πράξεις, specific actions; ἕξεις, dispositions (an Aristotelian ethical
term), reasoning, and the virtues themselves.

τῶν ἀρετῶν κάλλος. Εἰ δέ τι καὶ πρὸ τούτων, αὐτὸ δείξει.
Τί οὖν δὴ τὸ πεποιηκὸς καὶ τὰ σώματα καλὰ φαντάζεσθαι
καὶ τὴν ἀκοὴν ἐπινεύειν ταῖς φωναῖς, ὡς καλαί; Καὶ ὅσα
ἐφεξῆς ψυχῆς ἔχεται, πῶς ποτε πάντα καλά; Καὶ ἆρά γε
ἑνὶ καὶ τῷ αὐτῷ καλῷ τὰ πάντα, ἢ ἄλλο μὲν ἐν σώματι τὸ   10
κάλλος, ἄλλο δὲ ἐν ἄλλῳ; Καὶ τίνα ποτὲ ταῦτα ἢ τοῦτο;
Τὰ μὲν γὰρ οὐ παρ' αὐτῶν τῶν ὑποκειμένων καλά, οἷον τὰ
σώματα, ἀλλὰ μεθέξει, τὰ δὲ κάλλη αὐτά, ὥσπερ ἀρετῆς ἡ
φύσις. Σώματα μὲν γὰρ τὰ αὐτὰ ὁτὲ μὲν καλά, ὁτὲ δὲ οὐ

1,6. αὐτὸ: αὐτὸ τὸ καλόν. Beauty at a higher level is self-manifesting. We search for it, but in the end it is not just our own searching but the active self-manifestation of the ultimate Beauty that makes it accessible to us. Elsewhere Plotinus speaks of the self-manifestation of the One that, like the sun's rising, we must patiently await (5.5.8,3–5).

1,7. φαντάζεσθαι. Probably middle ("imagine"), since the objects here are seen from the perspective of the perceiving faculties (sight, hearing) rather than from their objective existence, which would require the passive meaning "appear," as in 4,10.

1,8. καλαί. Nominative, as εἰσί is understood. It would be wrong to "correct" to καλαῖς, as some editors do.

1,9. ἔχεσθαι (middle) + genitive: "to be concerned with," "appertain to"; ἐφεξῆς is an adverb, "directly."

1,12–13. ὑποκειμένων is another example of an Aristotelian term, used here together with the notion of "participation," μέθεξις, which is developed from Plato's description of particulars as participating in a Form (*Parm.* 132d3)

1,13. Plotinus uses the noun κάλλη "beauties" here rather than the substantive formed from the neuter plural of the adjective (καλά) because, as we will see later in the treatise, virtues at the intellectual level do not "share" in beauty as an attribute but have it as an essential element of their reality (see 6,21–22).

καλὰ φαίνεται, ὡς ἄλλου ὄντος τοῦ σώματα εἶναι, ἄλλου   15
δὲ τοῦ καλά. Τί οὖν ἐστι τοῦτο τὸ παρὸν τοῖς σώμασι;
Πρῶτον γὰρ περὶ τούτου σκεπτέον. Τί οὖν ἐστιν, ὃ κινεῖ
τὰς ὄψεις τῶν θεωμένων καὶ ἐπιστρέφει πρὸς αὐτὸ καὶ ἕλκει
καὶ εὐφραίνεσθαι τῇ θέᾳ ποιεῖ; Τοῦτο γὰρ εὑρόντες τάχ᾽ ἂν
ἐπιβάθρᾳ αὐτῷ χρώμενοι καὶ τὰ ἄλλα θεασαίμεθα. Λέ-   20
γεται μὲν δὴ παρὰ πάντων, ὡς εἰπεῖν, ὡς συμμετρία τῶν μερῶν πρὸς ἄλληλα καὶ πρὸς τὸ ὅλον τό τε τῆς εὐχροίας προστε-

1,15–16. τὸ σώματα εἶναι, τὸ καλὰ εἶναι: "their being bodies, their being beautiful"

1,18. ἐπιστρέφει. The idea of turning inward and upward (ἐπιστροφή) is one of Plotinus's key metaphysical concepts. Each level of reality is not only generated by its prior but also has its own power of turning upward to contemplate its cause and, in so doing, to perfect itself. The hypostases do this always, whereas the individual soul only intermittently and with great effort, but its spiritual excellence depends on this effort. Here, however, the power of turning back is actively ascribed to the cause, beauty. The initial impact of beauty evokes a passive response, but in the following two chapters Plotinus describes how we begin to respond in an increasingly active manner.

1,20. See Plato, *Symp.* 211c3: ὥσπερ ἐπαναβασμοῖς χρώμενον. The citation is adapted to the syntax, and the use of ἐπιβάθρᾳ might suggest a confusion with βάθρῳ cited in 9,15 from *Phaedr.* 254b7. But it should be noted that references to Plato are made at different levels; sometimes the exact wording is deemed to be important, at other times stylistic adjustments are made or, where the exact wording is less important, the reference serves simply to remind us of a particular passage. Lastly, there are many instances of Platonic reminiscences that occur to him quite naturally and almost subconsciously.

1,21. ὡς εἰπεῖν qualifies πάντων "virtually all." For the definition of beauty as a combination of symmetry and color, see Plato, *Soph.* 235e6–7 and the Stoic theory as found in Cicero, *Tusc.* 4.31. Plotinus hesitates (ὡς εἰπεῖν) because he will go on to argue that the true Platonic analysis goes deeper than this.

θὲν τὸ πρὸς τὴν ὄψιν κάλλος ποιεῖ καὶ ἔστιν αὐτοῖς καὶ ὅλως
τοῖς ἄλλοις πᾶσι τὸ καλοῖς εἶναι τὸ συμμέτροις καὶ μεμετρημένοις ὑπάρχειν· οἷς ἁπλοῦν οὐδέν, μόνον δὲ τὸ σύνθετον   25
ἐξ ἀνάγκης καλὸν ὑπάρξει· τό τε ὅλον ἔσται καλὸν αὐτοῖς,
τὰ δὲ μέρη ἕκαστα οὐχ ἕξει παρ' ἑαυτῶν τὸ καλὰ εἶναι,
πρὸς δὲ τὸ ὅλον συντελοῦντα, ἵνα καλὸν ᾖ· καίτοι δεῖ,
εἴπερ ὅλον, καὶ τὰ μέρη καλὰ εἶναι· οὐ γὰρ δὴ ἐξ
αἰσχρῶν, ἀλλὰ πάντα κατειληφέναι τὸ κάλλος. Τά τε   30
χρώματα αὐτοῖς τὰ καλά, οἷον καὶ τὸ τοῦ ἡλίου φῶς, ἁπλᾶ
ὄντα, οὐκ ἐκ συμμετρίας ἔχοντα τὸ κάλλος ἔξω ἔσται
τοῦ καλὰ εἶναι. Χρυσός τε δὴ πῶς καλόν; Καὶ νυκτὸς ἡ
ἀστραπὴ ἢ ἄστρα ὁρᾶσθαι τῷ καλά; Ἐπί τε τῶν φωνῶν

1,24–25. καλοῖς, συμμέτροις καὶ μεμετρημένοις. The datives refer back to αὐτοῖς ... τοῖς ἄλλοις πᾶσι (1,23–34).

1,25. οἷς refers to πάντων (1,21).

1,30. πάντα here is probably the object, but it is also possible to make it the subject (so Armstrong). καταλαμβάνω, however, seems to be used by Plotinus more in the sense of the higher taking hold of and molding the lower; see 2,24 and 3.2.4, where λόγος takes hold of matter.

1,31. Plotinus's solution will be found in 3,17–18, where he explains that color is produced by light, which is a form.

αὐτοῖς. See on 1,24–25.

1,32. The two participles are not parallel, but the second depends logically on the first.

1,34. The whole sentence is difficult and may be corrupt. The manuscript has καλῶ. I suggest reading indefinite τῳ (τινι) and καλά. ὁρᾶσθαι is passive rather than middle: "beautiful to be beheld by anyone."

Theiler objects to ἄστρα on the grounds that the stars are not simple undifferentiated objects like color but complex (he cleverly suggests that ἄστρα may be an error of the copyist [dittography] in repeating two syllables from ἀστραπή). However, single stars may be seen as simple points

ὡσαύτως τὸ ἁπλοῦν οἰχήσεται, καίτοι ἑκάστου φθόγγου   35
πολλαχῇ τῶν ἐν τῷ ὅλῳ καλῷ καλοῦ καὶ αὐτοῦ ὄντος.
Ὅταν δὲ δὴ καὶ τῆς αὐτῆς συμμετρίας μενούσης ὁτὲ μὲν
καλὸν τὸ αὐτὸ πρόσωπον, ὁτὲ δὲ μὴ φαίνηται, πῶς οὐκ
ἄλλο δεῖ ἐπὶ τῷ συμμέτρῳ λέγειν τὸ καλὸν εἶναι, καὶ
τὸ σύμμετρον καλὸν εἶναι δι’ ἄλλο; Εἰ δὲ δὴ μετα-   40
βαίνοντες καὶ ἐπὶ τὰ ἐπιτηδεύματα καὶ τοὺς λόγους τοὺς
καλοὺς τὸ σύμμετρον καὶ ἐπ’ αὐτῶν αἰτιῷντο, τίς ἂν
λέγοιτο ἐν ἐπιτηδεύμασι συμμετρία καλοῖς ἢ νόμοις ἢ
μαθήμασιν ἢ ἐπιστήμαις; Θεωρήματα γὰρ σύμμετρα πρὸς
ἄλληλα πῶς ἂν εἴη; Εἰ δ’ ὅτι σύμφωνά ἐστι, καὶ κακῶν   45
ἔσται ὁμολογία τε καὶ συμφωνία. Τῷ γὰρ τὴν σωφροσύ-
νην ἠλιθιότητα εἶναι τὸ τὴν δικαιοσύνην γενναίαν

---

of light, and, if the objection is that stars are beautiful because of their appearance in constellations, a similar objection could be raised against Plotinus's example of the single note, which, it could be argued, acquires its particular characteristic by its relationship to other notes. Plotinus may also be thinking here of Venus, the evening and morning star (to which he refers in 4,11–12), which at first appears alone in the night sky.

1,39–40. Note the chiasmus here. See the introduction above, p. 19.

1,41. Cf. Plato, *Symp.* 210d5: καλοὺς λόγους; 211a7: οὐδέ τις λόγος οὐδέ τις ἐπιστήμη.

1,43. Cf. the sequence σώματα, ἐπιτηδεύματα, μαθήματα in Plato, *Symp.* 211c5–6; for νόμοι, see *Symp.* 210c4

1,44. θεώρημα may mean "object of contemplation" in a metaphysical sense, but here, as often, it means "proposition."

1,46–47. Both of these propositions are taken from Plato (*Resp.* (560d2–3, 348c11–12; for the first, see also *Gorg.* 491e2), who, of course, does not accept them. Plotinus's point is that the concordance of two false propositions does not mean that they are true (and therefore καλόν).

εἶναι εὐήθειαν σύμφωνον καὶ συνῳδὸν καὶ ὁμολογεῖ πρὸς
ἄλληλα. Κάλλος μὲν οὖν ψυχῆς ἀρετὴ πᾶσα καὶ κάλλος
ἀληθινώτερον ἢ τὰ πρόσθεν· ἀλλὰ πῶς σύμμετρα; Οὔτε γὰρ   50
ὡς μεγέθη οὔτε ὡς ἀριθμὸς σύμμετρα· καὶ πλειόνων μερῶν
τῆς ψυχῆς ὄντων, ἐν ποίῳ γὰρ λόγῳ ἡ σύνθεσις ἢ ἡ κρᾶσις
τῶν μερῶν ἢ τῶν θεωρημάτων; Τὸ δὲ τοῦ νοῦ κάλλος
μονουμένου τί ἂν εἴη;

1,51. μερῶν. μέρος is often used by Platonists to differentiate powers of the
soul. This does not imply that the soul has "parts" in the physical sense.
Plotinus would have in mind not only the Platonic "tripartite" division
of soul (*Resp.* 435a-444e) but also the Aristotelian distinction of soul faculties (growth, sensation, reason, etc.) that he incorporated into his own
thought. For Plotinus's amalgamation of Platonic and Aristotelian elements in his psychology, see Blumenthal 1971, 1972.

Chapter 2

Plotinus now explains the way in which our active engagement with beauty takes place at the very lowest level, the encounter with physical beauty, which then leads (2,11–28) to the question of how the beauty in physical objects relates to the beauty of incorporeals. His solution involves an explication of the relationship of form to matter, and here he goes well beyond the relatively simple Platonic concept of participation, that multiple physical objects can share in a single transcendent Form, to present a more dynamic notion of the way in which form imposes itself on matter. All of this involves brief reference to a number of complex philosophical ideas that are more fully dealt with in other treatises: the relationship of form to matter (2.5 and 6), the nature of soul and how we perceive (4.1–9), and the designation of matter as evil (1.8; 2.4).

2. Πάλιν οὖν ἀναλαβόντες λέγωμεν τί δῆτά ἐστι τὸ ἐν
τοῖς σώμασι καλὸν πρῶτον. Ἔστι μὲν γάρ τι καὶ βολῇ τῇ
πρώτῃ αἰσθητὸν γινόμενον καὶ ἡ ψυχὴ ὥσπερ συνεῖσα λέγει
καὶ ἐπιγνοῦσα ἀποδέχεται καὶ οἷον συναρμόττεται. Πρὸς

2,1. δῆτα is a strengthened form of δή, a favorite particle of Plotinus ("in fact, really"), to mark the return to the question about the cause of physical beauty after the elimination of traditional inadequate theories.

2,3. συνεῖσα: aorist participle of συνίημι "understand."

λέγει. In 3.5.1,18 the σύνεσις that the soul has of its own "likeness" to what is perceived in this primary awareness of beauty is said to be ἄλογος. But this need not contradict λέγει here, since ἄλογος refers to the inchoate and not fully rationalized act of perception that does, nevertheless, make an affirmation of some kind. See Emilsson 1988, 125, who refers to 6.3.18,7–11, where, in distinguishing colors, Plotinus says "it is either sense perception or intellect that *says* that they are different, and they will not give a reason [λόγος], sense perception because the reason [λόγος] does not belong to it, but only giving different indications [μνημύσεις]." Here we have the same apparent paradox that excludes λόγος but admits λέγειν.

2,4. συναρμόττεται. Here middle, "fitting to itself." Cf. 3,3–4 of the soul, which is said συναρμόττουσα τῷ παρ᾽ αὐτῇ εἴδει, where we need to supply the object τὸ καλὸν σῶμα, and the similar idea expressed a little further (line 14), of comparing and fitting the external perception to an internal standard. The complete import of this will only gradually be fully explained in the context of what is beautiful. In fact, it is a general principle in Plotinus that all perception is brought to completion by the comparison of the external originating percept with the ideal forms, which exist in the soul. But now a further factor comes into play. Since, as we will later learn, all form is beautiful, perception is always of form, and the formless is "perceived" or recognized only by its absence. Ugliness, therefore, is not recognized in the same way as beauty, and this is also seen by the fact that we recoil from ugliness but are attracted by beauty, since the former is not like the form within us, whereas what is beautiful is akin to form within the soul.

Note the qualifications ὥσπερ, οἷον (2,3–4). This is only the first, preliminary, and incomplete stage in the recognition of beauty, which is

δὲ τὸ αἰσχρὸν προσβαλοῦσα ἀνίλλεται καὶ ἀρνεῖται καὶ   5
ἀνανεύει ἀπ' αὐτοῦ οὐ συμφωνοῦσα καὶ ἀλλοτριουμένη.

---

developed further in the next chapter and to its highest level in what follows. Plotinus has carefully observed that initial and almost instinctive
attraction we feel toward what is beautiful and our corresponding aver-
sion from what is ugly. For many, the reaction to beauty will go no further
than this. But although true beauty and happiness will be found at a much
deeper level, we are not to belittle these primary stirrings. In fact, this
immediate awareness of beauty is, for Plotinus, an important insight into
the way in which we begin to access the intelligible world. We may note the
cognitive processes involved (qualified as noted above): λέγει (expressing),
σύνεσις (understanding), ἐπίγνωσις (recognition), ἁρμόζειν (fitting). This
should be compared with the description in the next chapter where the
process proceeds with the involvement of "the rest of soul" (ἡ ἄλλη ψυχή,
i.e., other than the lower faculty of immediate perception), which is said
to assist in making judgments, and the forms within the soul are explicitly
invoked. The state of primary awareness is described in similar terms in
3.5.1,17–18. For ἐπίγνωσις, see also 2.916,45; 4.4.5,16, and 5.3.2,11–12.
     That some kind of judgment (κρίσις) is involved even at this stage is
implied by the statement in the following chapter (3,3) that the rest of the
soul "joins with it in judging" (συνεπικρίνει). For Plotinus, all perceptions
involve some form of judgment from the very moment that the sensory
affection is detected (see Emilsson 1988, 121–25).

2,5. ἀνίλλεται: "shrinks back." The word is used by Plato (*Symp.* 206d6),
where he refers to the soul's antipathy to ugliness.

2,6. ἀλλοτριουμένη. See also 1.6.6,17 and 3.6.1,21, in both cases coupled
with οἰκείωσις (appropriation). Behind these expressions lies the Stoic
idea that the individual instinctively affirms and accepts what is according to his nature while rejecting what is alien. See Long and Sedley 1987,
1:346–54. But Plotinus modifies the Stoic doctrine in two ways. First,
while accepting that the Good is οἰκεῖον to the soul (6.5.1,16–21), he qualifies this (6.7.27) to affirm that it is οἰκεῖον because it is good, but one may
not say that it is good because it is οἰκεῖον. This nonreciprocal affirmation
ensures the transcendence at each level of the object for which one strives.
Similarly, each level of reality is akin to what is above it, but what is above

Φαμὲν δή, ὡς τὴν φύσιν οὖσα ὅπερ ἐστὶ καὶ πρὸς τῆς
κρείττονος ἐν τοῖς οὖσιν οὐσίας, ὅ τι ἂν ἴδη συγγενὲς ἢ
ἴχνος τοῦ συγγενοῦς, χαίρει τε καὶ διεπτόηται καὶ
ἀναφέρει πρὸς ἑαυτὴν καὶ ἀναμιμνήσκεται ἑαυτῆς καὶ τῶν   10
ἑαυτῆς. Τίς οὖν ὁμοιότης τοῖς τῆδε πρὸς τὰ ἐκεῖ καλά;
καὶ γάρ, εἰ ὁμοιότης, ὅμοια μὲν ἔστω· πῶς δὲ καλὰ κἀκεῖνα
καὶ ταῦτα; Μετοχῇ εἴδους φαμὲν ταῦτα. Πᾶν μὲν γὰρ τὸ
ἄμορφον πεφυκὸς μορφὴν καὶ εἶδος δέχεσθαι ἄμοιρον ὂν
λόγου καὶ εἴδους αἰσχρὸν καὶ ἔξω θείου λόγου· καὶ τὸ πάντη   15

---

is not akin, in the same sense, to what is beneath it. Second, while allowing
that soul and intellect may have a natural propensity to belong to or turn
to themselves, this cannot be said of the Good or the One, which does not
turn to itself but is good only to others (6.7.41,28–29).

2,7. φύσιν: accusative of respect with οὖσα. The phrase πρὸς ... οὐσίας (2,7–
8) should also be taken with οὖσα. The latter phrase refers to intellect, and
οὐσία is used in the generic sense of incorporeal reality, which includes
both soul and intellect. Elsewhere οὐσία may be used more strictly of Intellect seen as the realm of Forms, which are real being in the full sense.

2,8. ὅ τι ἂν...: to be taken as the object of χαίρει.

2,9. τοῦ συγγενοῦς. For the kinship of soul to the divine, see Plato, *Phaed.*
79d3. Relevant also here is the traditional doctrine, held also by Plato, that
like is perceived by like (see Plato, *Tim.* 37a–c and Aristotle's interpretation of the doctrine in *De an.* 404b17, 405b15–19). See also *Enn.* 1.8.1,8,
2.4.10,3.

2,11. ἐκεῖ is frequently used by Plotinus to indicate the transcendent world
of Intellect and so may be translated here as "the intelligible world," as contrasted with "the physical universe" (τὰ τῇδε).

2,13–15. αἰσχρὸν ... λόγου is predicate (ἐστί is omitted) to the subject πᾶν
τὸ ἄμορφον. πεφυκός and ὄν, two participles describing τὸ ἄμορφον, have different functions; the former is attributive (πεφυκός ... δέχεσθαι), the latter
adverbial: "*as long as* it is without a share of reason principle and form."

αἰσχρὸν τοῦτο. Αἰσχρὸν δὲ καὶ τὸ μὴ κρατηθὲν ὑπὸ
μορφῆς καὶ λόγου οὐκ ἀνασχομένης τῆς ὕλης τὸ πάντῃ

2,13–16. πᾶν μὲν … τοῦτο. These lines refer to matter (ὕλη), which for Plotinus is without any form; nor is it simply something without or deprived of form but is privation itself. For this reason it is τὸ <u>πάντῃ</u> αἰσχρόν. The following lines (αἰσχρὸν δὲ…) refer to bodies, that is, combinations of matter and a limited amount of form (τὸ πάντῃ κατὰ τὸ εἶδος μορφοῦσθαι) and that are therefore ugly insofar as they share only partially in form. Presumably such bodies may also manifest some aspects of beauty insofar as they have some share in form. Moreover, Plotinus considers prime matter (matter without any attributes conferred by form) to be not only complete ugliness but also evil and the cause of evil—not, of course, of moral evil, which is the responsibility of the individual, but of lack of order or beauty in the universe. However, the evil presented by matter remains still of prime concern for the individual because it provides the environment that so easily overwhelms the soul, if it does not resist it, and moral failure is, precisely, our submission to its allure.

2,15. λόγου καὶ εἴδους. λόγος, εἶδος, and μορφή have each a slightly different nuance. μορφή suggests what is manifest or perceptible; εἶδος, in the present context, is the standard Platonic notion of form, whether viewed as immanent or transcendent; λόγος has a wide range of meanings, including "reason," "argument," "expression." In this context, as so often, it has a meaning similar to that of εἶδος but brings with it the implication of subordination, that each level of reality is an expression or image of that above it, as they unfold from the highest level in Intellect to the lowest embodied instance. This usage is sometimes translated "reason principle": *principle* to indicate its causal force, and *reason* to indicate rationality and order, properties that are implied by the root word λέγειν, for a λόγος is the expressed product of rational thought. εἶδος, on the other hand, suggests more the notion of image. It should be emphasized that all three, particularly εἶδος and λόγος, are conceived as active powers and entities in their own right.

2,16. καί: "also," that is, as well as the total lack of form mentioned in the previous sentence.

κατὰ τὸ εἶδος μορφοῦσθαι. Προσιὸν οὖν τὸ εἶδος τὸ μὲν
ἐκ πολλῶν ἐσόμενον μερῶν ἓν συνθέσει συνέταξέ τε καὶ
εἰς μίαν συντέλειαν ἤγαγε καὶ ἐν τῇ ὁμολογίᾳ πεποίηκεν,   20
ἐπείπερ ἓν ἦν αὐτὸ ἕν τε ἔδει τὸ μορφούμενον εἶναι ὡς
δυνατὸν αὐτῷ ἐκ πολλῶν ὄντι. Ἵδρυται οὖν ἐπ' αὐτοῦ τὸ
κάλλος ἤδη εἰς ἓν συναχθέντος καὶ τοῖς μέρεσι διδὸν ἑαυτὸ
καὶ τοῖς ὅλοις. Ὅταν δὲ ἕν τι καὶ ὁμοιομερὲς καταλάβῃ,
εἰς ὅλον δίδωσι τὸ αὐτό· οἷον ὁτὲ μὲν πάσῃ οἰκίᾳ μετὰ   25
τῶν μερῶν, ὁτὲ δὲ ἑνὶ λίθῳ διδοίη τις φύσις τὸ κάλλος, τῇ
δὲ ἡ τέχνη. Οὕτω μὲν δὴ τὸ καλὸν σῶμα γίγνεται λόγου

2,18. μὲν. The beauty of things composed of different parts is compared (δὲ, 2,24) with the beauty of single entities, whose parts are identical with each other and the whole, thus concluding the argument of this chapter that form is the cause of beauty with a reference back to the claim made in chapter 1 (against symmetry as a cause of beauty) that simple things can be beautiful.

2,21–22. We should notice here the importance of unity in the transmission of beauty through form. Ultimately the One, as cause of all, is the cause of unity and coherence. We should not then be surprised that the role of the One is briefly touched upon at the end of the treatise in the discussion whether Intellect or the One is to be identified with beauty itself.

2,26–27. τῇ δὲ ἡ τέχνη refers back as subject to ὁτὲ … μερῶν (understand διδοίη). It is added almost as an afterthought. But that need not surprise us, since the distinction often made by Plotinus between art and nature (see 5.8.1–2) is not strictly relevant to his argument here, where his primary concern is to note that beauty brings unity both to complex things made up of different parts and to simple things, any part of which is qualitatively the same as the whole, for instance, gold or, as here, a stone. Simple objects have already been mentioned in the argument in chapter 1 that beauty does not consist in symmetry.

2,27. μὲν is to be taken with the initial δὲ of the following chapter (the chapter divisions of modern editions were first made by Ficino). It marks the progression from the first basic argument that form is the cause of

ἀπὸ θείων ἐλθόντος κοινωνίᾳ.

---

order and beauty to a more intricate analysis of how this is perceived and exploited by the human soul.

2,28. θείων. Understand εἴδων. Cf. 2,15.

Chapter 3

The simple awareness of beauty is taken further. The soul now invokes its higher powers to acquire a better grasp of beauty by comparing its sense-impressions with the forms, which it already has within it from intellect. It is for this reason that Plotinus now goes into further detail about the relationship of the forms within soul (and the transcendent forms within our intellect) with the forms embodied in the objects of perception that sense-perception provides; consequently, there is further consideration of the relationship of embodied and transcendent form and the way in which the former is experienced by the soul. The discussion of embodied form then extends beyond external shape to include color, which is treated as a physical manifestation different from that of shape, and sound. The addition of hearing (3,28–33) rounds off the discussion of the types of physical beauty (sight and sound) announced at the beginning of the treatise and that all require matter for their manifestation (3,33–36).

3. Γινώσκει δὲ αὐτὸ ἡ ἐπ' αὐτῷ δύναμις τεταγμένη, ἧς
οὐδὲν κυριώτερον εἰς κρίσιν τῶν ἑαυτῆς, ὅταν καὶ ἡ ἄλλη
συνεπικρίνῃ ψυχή· τάχα δὲ καὶ αὕτη λέγῃ συναρμόττουσα

3,1. Note the emphasis placed on γινώσκει as first word in the sentence.

αὐτὸ: τὸ κάλλος, 2,23 and 26. αὐτῷ: the process of perceiving beauty described in 2,1–11.

3,1–5. ἡ ἐπ' αὐτῷ δύναμις τεταγμένη is that aspect of the soul whose operations are described in chapter 2. But Plotinus implies here that its powers of discernment are augmented (κυριώτερον εἰς κρίσιν) when it works together with the higher faculties of the soul, which are indicated by the phrase ἡ ἄλλη ... ψυχή. The "rest of the soul" may be identified with the more complex operations that are the sphere of discursive reason. A similar division may be seen in 5.3.3,1–2, where sense-perception is said to "give its impression [τύπος] of a sense-object to discursive reason [διάνοια]." A little later (5.3.4,15–17) we learn that discursive reason understands (σύνεσις) external objects and judges them by means of standards (κανόσιν) within itself, which it has acquired from intellect.

αὕτη (3,3) would seem also to refer to the lower powers of soul, which here, as in chapter 2, are accorded some measure of active cognition. But Plotinus is careful to qualify this (τάχα: "perhaps"). The ascription of such powers, even in rudimentary form, to the lower soul is clearly problematical, and while Plotinus wants to indicate that humans have a built-in or innate sense of beauty, he wishes at the same time to avoid overcomplicating his exposition at this point. Thus the vagueness of his account is to be explained by his unwillingness to overburden the main point he is making here (our experience of *beauty*) with the difficult questions involved in trying to clarify exactly how a transmission is possible from the sense-object to discursive reason, questions that are properly dealt with in the context of sense-perception. Note that Theiler (Harder, Beutler, and Theiler 1956–1971), Blumenthal (1971, 105 n. 12), and others reject Henry and Schwyzer's interpretation of αὕτη as referring to ἡ ἄλλη ψυχή and instead read αὐτὴ, which makes the reference to δύναμις more obvious.

3,3–4. A direct object (e.g., ὅ τι ἂν ἴδῃ) must be supplied to συναρμόττουσα.

τῷ παρ᾽ αὐτῇ εἴδει κἀκείνῳ πρὸς τὴν κρίσιν χρωμένη ὥσπερ
κανόνι τοῦ εὐθέος. Πῶς δὲ συμφωνεῖ τὸ περὶ σῶμα τῷ πρὸ   5
σώματος; Πῶς δὲ τὴν ἔξω οἰκίαν τῷ ἔνδον οἰκίας εἴδει ὁ
οἰκοδομικὸς συναρμόσας καλὴν εἶναι λέγει; Ἢ ὅτι ἐστὶ τὸ
ἔξω, εἰ χωρίσειας τοὺς λίθους, τὸ ἔνδον εἶδος μερισθὲν τῷ
ἔξω ὕλης ὄγκῳ, ἀμερὲς ὂν ἐν πολλοῖς φανταζόμενον. Ὅταν

παρ᾽ αὐτῇ: the form that it has in itself. See the note on reflexives in the text of Plotinus, page 19 in the introduction above.

ἐκείνῳ (κἀκείνῳ = καὶ ἐκείνῳ) is object to χρωμένη.

3,5. κανόνι. For the image of the ruler, see also 1.8.9,3, 4.4.23,39, and 5.3.4,16.

3,6–9. τὴν ἔξω οἰκίαν may most easily be understood as indicating the physical house together with its immanent form, while τῷ ἔνδον οἰκίας εἴδει is the form within the builder. But in the next sentence the phrase τὸ ἔνδον εἶδος appears to refer to the form immanent in the house rather than in the builder. Plotinus seems here to be identifying the external manifestation (τὸ ἔξω [εἶδος?]) with the form immanent in the house, except insofar as the former is "divided" by matter, that is, strictly speaking undivided but being manifested (φανταζόμενον) as divided. It is because of this undivided nature that the builder or anyone who perceives the house can make the comparison and fit the form received from the external object with the form already within the soul.

3,8–9. τῷ ἔξω ὕλης ὄγκῳ. Matter, for Plotinus, has no qualities and is to be identified with total deprivation. It is the facilitator of three-dimensionality in the sense that form may, by being reflected on it as on a mirror, create the manifestation of a three-dimensional world. In this sense matter enables the existence of "mass" (ὄγκος), which is the most basic representation of three-dimensionality before the imposition of more specific forms.

ἀμερὲς ... φανταζόμενον. Even form as present to matter is partless in the sense of physically discrete parts but is manifested as having parts. Accordingly, the physical world of our experience, though not an illusion, may be regarded as a mere appearance in the sense of a reflection, and its

οὖν καὶ ἡ αἴσθησις τὸ ἐν σώμασιν εἶδος ἴδῃ συνδησάμενον   10
καὶ κρατῆσαν τῆς φύσεως τῆς ἐναντίας ἀμόρφου οὔσης
καὶ μορφὴν ἐπὶ ἄλλαις μορφαῖς ἐκπρεπῶς ἐποχουμένην,
συνελοῦσα ἀθρόον αὐτὸ τὸ πολλαχῇ ἀνήνεγκέ τε καὶ εἰσήγαγεν
εἰς τὸ εἴσω ἀμερὲς ἤδη καὶ ἔδωκε τῷ ἔνδον σύμφωνον καὶ
συναρμόττον καὶ φίλον· οἷα ἀνδρὶ ἀγαθῷ προσηνὲς ἐπιφαινό-   15
μενον ἀρετῆς ἴχνος ἐν νέῳ συμφωνοῦν τῷ ἀληθεῖ τῷ ἔνδον.
Τὸ δὲ τῆς χρόας κάλλος ἁπλοῦν μορφῇ καὶ κρατήσει τοῦ

---

three-dimensionality is due to matter reflecting the partless nature of form in three dimensions and thus diminished in nature.

3,14. ἀμερὲς ἤδη. This phrase is construed by Laurent with εἰς τὸ εἴσω, that is, the inner (or higher) soul that is partless. I take it as referring to τὸ ἐν σώμασιν εἶδος, "the form in bodies," (line 10), as do Armstrong ("takes it in, now without parts") and Kalligas.

3,17–28. Plotinus follows Aristotle (*De an.* 418b14–17) and Alexander of Aphrodisias (*Comm. Arist.* 2.1 *De an.* 42,19–43) in believing light to be incorporeal. He also finds the doctrine in Plato, *Tim.* 39b4–5 and 55d (2.1.7,23–28). In 4.5.6,14 he regards light as an ἐνέργεια and in 6.4.7,31 as an incorporeal δύναμις; in 1.1.4,16 the soul is said to be present to the body like light in the sense that light itself remains unaffected by the body it illuminates. Light is, then, an activity similar to that of soul or form but not identical with them, just as fire, on a level lower than that of light, is also not a form but is like a form (τάξιν εἴδους … ἔχει, 3,20). Plotinus's theory of color is expressed here in a way that fits in with his general argument that beauty is caused at each level by a cause located at a higher level of reality. So fire possesses color "in a primary way" (πρώτως, 3,24), which is then passed on to the other elements.

3,17. τὸ δὲ τῆς χρόας.... The syntax is difficult, as a verb must be provided (κρατήσει could be taken as a verb, but this seems unlikely). I suggest giving the nouns μορφῇ and κρατήσει a verbal force: "And the simple beauty of color shapes and masters the darkness of matter." Armstrong supplies an unexpressed verb: "the simple beauty of colour *comes about* by shape and the mastery of the darkness in matter" (emphasis added). Laurent and Gerson understand it in a similar way, but Kalligas gives

ἐν ὕλῃ σκοτεινοῦ παρουσίᾳ φωτὸς ἀσωμάτου καὶ λόγου καὶ
εἴδους ὄντος. Ὅθεν καὶ τὸ πῦρ αὐτὸ παρὰ τὰ ἄλλα σώματα
καλόν, ὅτι τάξιν εἴδους πρὸς τὰ ἄλλα στοιχεῖα ἔχει, ἄνω   20
μὲν τῇ θέσει, λεπτότατον δὲ τῶν ἄλλων σωμάτων, ὡς ἐγγὺς
ὂν τοῦ ἀσωμάτου, μόνον δὲ αὐτὸ οὐκ εἰσδεχόμενον τὰ
ἄλλα· τὰ δ’ ἄλλα δέχεται αὐτό. Θερμαίνεται γὰρ ἐκεῖνα,
οὐ ψύχεται δὲ τοῦτο, κέχρωσταί τε πρώτως, τὰ δ’ ἄλλα
παρὰ τούτου τὸ εἶδος τῆς χρόας λαμβάνει. Λάμπει οὖν καὶ   25
στίλβει, ὡς ἂν εἶδος ὄν. Τὸ δὲ μὴ κρατοῦν ἐξίτηλον τῷ
φωτὶ γινόμενον οὐκέτι καλόν, ὡς ἂν τοῦ εἴδους τῆς χρόας

ἁπλοῦν its full predicative force and takes μορφῇ as modifying ἁπλοῦν and
τοῦ ... σκοτεινοῦ as objective genitive only to κρατήσει. He then supplies
two verbal phrases to mark the difference: "the beauty of colour *is* simple
with regard to its shape and *is the consequence* of mastering the darkness
of matter" (emphasis added). He thus avoids implying that the beauty of
color is caused by μορφή. Shape or extent could hardly be considered as
active causes of color. In fact, Plotinus elsewhere (2.8.1,12–17) suggests
that the awareness of spatial extent is only an incidental concomitant in
our perception of color. Of course, μορφή may be used here simply to indicate form as denoting a specific color rather than to shape or extension.

3,18. παρουσίᾳ φώτος ἀσωμάτου. In 4.5.7,37–49 Plotinus discusses the way
in which light transmits color, which is produced by the presence of light
projected onto matter. See Emilsson 1988, 52–55. In 2.4.5,7–12 we find
the same contrast between the light provided by form and the darkness of
matter. Colors are even described as being instances of light (χρόας φῶτα
ὄντα).

3,19–20. τὸ πῦρ αὐτὸ παρὰ τὰ ἄλλα σώματα καλόν. See Plato, *Tim.* 40a3–4
for the idea that fire is more beautiful and less corporeal than the other
three elements: earth, air, and water. But perhaps Plotinus is also equat-
ing τὸ πῦρ αὐτο with the sun that provides the light that transmits color to
physical objects.

3,26–27. τὸ μὴ κρατοῦν. Literally, "that which does not master." But it is
unclear to what it might refer in the preceding sentences
and, more generally, what entity Plotinus has in mind. I take it, along with

οὐ μετέχον ὅλου. Αἱ δὲ ἁρμονίαι αἱ ἐν ταῖς φωναῖς αἱ
ἀφανεῖς τὰς φανερὰς ποιήσασαι καὶ ταύτῃ τὴν ψυχὴν
σύνεσιν καλοῦ λαβεῖν ἐποίησαν, ἐν ἄλλῳ τὸ αὐτὸ   30

Theiler and Igal, as referring to fire. Does he, then, mean inferior manifestations of fire as opposed to the highest physical manifestation of fire,
the sun, which is the first manifestation of light, or does he mean that fire
ceases where there is no combustible material, as Igal seems to think in his
commentary on the passage? The former explanation may be supported
by Plotinus's discussion in 4.5.7 of the way in which light is emitted as the
external activity of a luminous body such as the sun. At a lower level, he
mentions the eye as an example of a luminous body that emits light. In the
case of some animals, this body may expand at night, emitting much light
and contract during the day so that the light is not emitted as strongly. It
may then be such a phenomenon that he has in mind with the phrase τὸ
μὴ κρατοῦν, that is, a luminous (fiery) body that has become smaller and
less powerful.

Armstrong, on the other hand, thinks it refers to dull and ugly colors
that sometimes look uglier in bright light and translates: "The inferior
thing which becomes faint and dull by the fire's light is not beautiful any
more." Kalligas, taking it as referring to perceptible objects that cannot
share in the form of color in a complete and perfect way, translates: "While
the thing that color does not master, but that fades with the light, is no
longer beautiful." Laurent translates: "Ce qui ne s'impose pas [par un éclat
particulier] s'efface devant sa lumière et paraît ne plus avoir de beauté."
A more radical solution (Volkmann and Ficino) is to correct κρατοῦν to
κρατούμενον, "what is not mastered," thus making the phrase refer to whatever is a substrate for light and color. MacKenna seems to extract the same
meaning even by keeping the active form: "And all that has resisted and
is but uncertainly held by its light remains outside of beauty." However,
κρατεῖν, at least in this treatise, refers to the power of form to impose itself
rather than the resistance or incapacity of a substrate to receive form.

3,28–31. Plotinus has more to say in 1.3.1,20–35 about the role of musical
sound in raising us toward transcendent beauty, where he says that the
musical person is seen to be easily moved by the beauty in sounds and is
led on from physical sounds perceived by the senses to the beauty of their
intelligible archetypes. His description of the music lover who is attracted

δεῖξαι. Παρακολουθεῖ δὲ ταῖς αἰσθηταῖς μετρεῖσθαι
ἀριθμοῖς ἐν λόγῳ οὐ παντί, ἀλλ' ὃς ἂν ᾖ δουλεύων εἰς
ποίησιν εἴδους εἰς τὸ κρατεῖν. Καὶ περὶ μὲν τῶν ἐν
αἰσθήσει καλῶν, ἃ δὴ εἴδωλα καὶ σκιαὶ οἷον ἐκδρα-
μοῦσαι εἰς ὕλην ἐλθοῦσαι ἐκόσμησάν τε καὶ διεπτόησαν   35
φανεῖσαι, τοσαῦτα.

---

by harmony but avoids its opposite provides a parallel with the lover of
beauty in 1.6 who recoils from what is ugly.

3,28. αἱ δὲ ἁρμονίαι … αἱ ἀφανεῖς. Perhaps an echo of Heraclitus DK B54:
ἁρμονίη ἀφανὴς φανερῆς κρείττων. For a general account of Plotinus's use
of the Presocratics, see Stamatellos 2007; on hidden harmony and logos,
2007, 162.

3,35. εἰς ὕλην ἐλθοῦσαι ἐκόσμησαν. In 2.4.5,18 matter is described as a νεκρὸν
κεκοσμημένον and εἴδωλον is used of the embodied form.

διεπτόησαν. This is a strong word since it seems generally to be used of a
violent or disturbing affection but is evidently used by Plotinus in a positive way, as he also employs it in the next chapter to describe the experience of grasping transcendent beauty (4,14).

Chapter 4

The transition is now made to the soul's experience of transparent beauty, which can be properly described only by those who have attained it. Nevertheless, all have some access to it, although only true lovers of beauty fully appreciate its power.

4. Περὶ δὲ τῶν προσωτέρω καλῶν, ἃ οὐκέτι αἴσθησις
ὁρᾶν εἴληχε, ψυχὴ δὲ ἄνευ ὀργάνων ὁρᾷ καὶ λέγει, ἀνα-
βαίνοντας δεῖ θεάσασθαι καταλιπόντας τὴν αἴσθησιν κάτω
περιμένειν. Ὥσπερ δὲ ἐπὶ τῶν τῆς αἰσθήσεως καλῶν οὐκ ἦν
περὶ αὐτῶν λέγειν τοῖς μήτε ἑωρακόσι μήθ᾽ ὡς καλῶν   5
ἀντειλημμένοις, οἷον εἴ τινες ἐξ ἀρχῆς τυφλοὶ γεγονότες,
τὸν αὐτὸν τρόπον οὐδὲ περὶ κάλλους ἐπιτηδευμάτων μὴ τοῖς
ἀποδεξαμένοις τὸ τῶν ἐπιτηδευμάτων καὶ ἐπιστημῶν καὶ
τῶν ἄλλων τῶν τοιούτων κάλλος, οὐδὲ περὶ ἀρετῆς φέγγους
τοῖς μηδὲ φαντασθεῖσιν ὡς καλὸν τὸ τῆς δικαιοσύνης   10
καὶ σωφροσύνης πρόσωπον, καὶ οὔτε ἕσπερος οὔτε ἑῷ-
ος οὕτω καλά. Ἀλλὰ δεῖ ἰδόντας μὲν εἶναι ᾧ ψυχὴ τὰ

4,7. οὐκ ἦν ... λέγειν (4,4–5) is also to be understood after οὐδέ in 4,7 and 9.

4,9. ἀρετῆς φέγγους. Cf. Plato, *Phaedr.* 250b1–3: δικαιοσύνης μὲν οὖν καὶ σωφροσύνης ... φέγγος.

4,11–12. οὔτε ἕσπερος οὔτε ἑῷος οὕτω καλά. Plotinus is citing Euripides, *Melannipe* frag. 486, to which Nauck (1854) also adds the words δικαιοσύνης πρόσωπον. The same lines are also found in 6.6.6,39 and are cited by Aristotle, *Eth. nic.* 1129b28–29). However, it is evident that Plotinus knows them from a source other than Aristotle, since he gives them in a fuller form, taken probably from Adrastos (see Kalligas *ad loc.*), a Peripatetic philosopher of the second century CE whose works were among those read in Plotinus's seminars, according to Porphyry (*Vit. Plot.* 14).

Understand ἀστήρ with ἕσπερος and ἑῷος. This quotation is added almost as an afterthought as in 6.6.6,39 but is peculiarly appropriate here after the mention of stars in 1.6.1,34.

4,12. ἀλλὰ δεῖ ἰδόντας μὲν εἶναι: "but there must be those who see by means of...." The force of δεῖ expresses the necessary existence of those who can see the transcendent, if we are to have knowledge of it. Plotinus goes on to explain that all humans do have some intimation of this kind of experience, even in their encounter with purely physical beauty as explained previously in chapter 2.

τοιαῦτα βλέπει, ἰδόντας δὲ ἡσθῆναι καὶ ἔκπληξιν λαβεῖν καὶ
πτοηθῆναι πολλῷ μᾶλλον ἢ ἐν τοῖς πρόσθεν, ἅτε ἀληθινῶν
ἤδη ἐφαπτομένους. Ταῦτα γὰρ δεῖ τὰ πάθη γενέσθαι περὶ
τὸ ὅ τι ἂν ᾖ καλόν, θάμβος καὶ ἔκπληξιν ἡδεῖαν καὶ πόθον
καὶ ἔρωτα καὶ πτόησιν μεθ᾽ ἡδονῆς. Ἔστι δὲ ταῦτα παθεῖν
καὶ πάσχουσιν αἱ ψυχαὶ καὶ περὶ τὰ μὴ ὁρώμενα πᾶσαι
μέν, ὡς εἰπεῖν, μᾶλλον μέντοι αἱ τούτων ἐρωτικώτεραι,

15

4,12–13. ᾧ ψυχὴ ... βλέπει, "by that with which the soul sees such things,"
refers to the higher part of the soul that contains the forms that enable it to
recognize beauty in both physical objects and the incorporeal beauty (of
virtue and knowledge) in others.

4,15. πάθη. See also παθεῖν and πάσχουσι a few lines below. Of course, the
soul does not in fact suffer affections, at least not in the same way as a physical body. If we use πάθη of soul we mean changes that are self-imposed,
as Plotinus explains in 3.6, "On the Impassibility of Things without Body."
But the words are deliberately chosen here by Plotinus to emphasize the
power of the experience of beauty at all levels.

4,16. τὸ ὅ τι. The use of the article with ὅστις seems unusual. But see Smyth
2532b for use with οἷος and ἡλίκος.

4,17. ἔρωτα. Love is mentioned here explicitly for the first time, thus introducing this important theme from Plato's *Symposium*. The theme is picked
up again at the beginning of the next chapter. For Plotinus, love expresses
that innate power and urge of all being, especially of the human individual, to return to its source.

ἔστι: "it is possible," impersonal use plus infinitive.

4,19. ὡς εἰπεῖν (literally "so as to say") may be taken with either πᾶσαι
(Armstrong and Laurent) or πάσχουσι (McKenna, Theiler, Kalligas), the
former meaning that "nearly all" humans have this experience, the latter
that all humans have it to some extent. This fits better the comparison with
physical seeing in the following lines that contrasts the fact that all "see"
with the different effects that sight has on them.
    The statement that all souls have some experience of true beauty may

ὥσπερ καὶ ἐπὶ τῶν σωμάτων πάντες μὲν ὁρῶσι, κεν-   20
τοῦνται δ' οὐκ ἴσα, ἀλλ' εἰσὶν οἳ μάλιστα, οἳ καὶ λέγονται
ἐρᾶν.

---

seem surprising, since it implies that all humans have some insight into
intelligible beauty. Behind this may lie the consideration that even physical
beauty could not be acknowledged unless we have some kind of experience, however faint, of its transcendent cause. A similarly positive view
is implied in the assertion (1.6.8,26–27) that we all have the possibility of
seeing the intelligible, though few actually achieve it.

4,20–22. All are smitten (κεντοῦνται) but not in equal measure. The relative clause οἳ καὶ λέγονται ἐρᾶν "those who are also said to be in love" is
not contrasted with, but describes in different terms, those who are most
affected (εἰσὶν οἳ μάλιστα).

Chapter 5

Plotinus continues the description of our experience of transcendent beauty, stressing the personal encounter with the use of the second-person and its powerful effect on us (ἀναβακχεύεσθε, ἀνακινεῖσθε, ποθεῖτε). The tone then changes from line 8 (use of the third-person) and the following lines that introduce a more objective and analytical examination. The transition is also here made from the observation of moral beauty in the actions of others to the inner beauty of their souls and of our own soul. This internal beauty is then identified with being, a key metaphysical concept of the treatise. The rest of the chapter is then devoted to an important discursive approach to our understanding of beauty through our recognition of the nature of its opposite, ugliness. The subtle mixture and balancing of personal experience and discursive analysis, as displayed in this chapter, is a fundamental characteristic of Plotinus's philosophical method.

5. Τῶν δὴ καὶ περὶ τὰ ἐν οὐκ αἰσθήσει ἐρωτικῶν
ἀναπυνθάνεσθαι δεῖ· τί πάσχετε περὶ τὰ λεγόμενα ἐπιτηδεύματα καλὰ καὶ τρόπους καλοὺς καὶ ἤθη σώφρονα
καὶ ὅλως ἔργα ἀρετῆς καὶ διαθέσεις καὶ τὸ τῶν ψυχῶν
κάλλος; Καὶ ἑαυτοὺς δὲ ἰδόντες τὰ ἔνδον καλοὺς τί   5
πάσχετε; Καὶ πῶς ἀναβακχεύεσθε καὶ ἀνακινεῖσθε καὶ
ἑαυτοῖς συνεῖναι ποθεῖτε συλλεξάμενοι αὐτοὺς ἀπὸ τῶν
σωμάτων; Πάσχουσι μὲν γὰρ ταῦτα οἱ ὄντως ἐρωτικοί. Τί
δέ ἐστι, περὶ ὃ ταῦτα πάσχουσιν; Οὐ σχῆμα, οὐ χρῶμα,

5,1. ἀναπυνθάνομαι (5,2) may take the genitive of the person questioned.

Note καὶ qualifying the "lovers of nonsensibles." Plotinus does not want to disregard their love of physical beauty.

5,5. τὰ ἔνδον is to be taken as accusative of respect with καλοὺς: "what do you experience when you look at yourselves, beautiful within."
    We have already been alerted (2,10–11) to the idea that the soul contains beauty because it has within it the forms that enable it to recognize physical beauty. But now the emphasis is on the beauty of virtues rather than of the forms of beautiful objects. For internal beauty, see Plato, *Phaedr.* 279b9.

5,6–7. Note how Plotinus expresses his questions dramatically, using the second-person. This vivid use of direct speech is characteristic of Plotinus's "teaching" style as he tries to engage his students in the task of introspection.

ἀναβακχεύεσθε has the strong meaning of being "stirred up in a Bacchic frenzy." It is found again in 6.7.22,9, also in the context of "love" at the highest level when the soul receives an "outflow" from the One that "arouses" it to mystical union (ψυχὴ λαβοῦσα εἰς αὐτὴν τὴν ἐκεῖθεν ἀπορροὴν κινεῖται καὶ ἀναβακχεύεται καὶ οἴστρων πίμπλαται καὶ ἔρως γίνεται).
    The appeal to a more emotionally and subjectively based experience in these opening lines alerts us to Plotinus's complex understanding of introspection, which is both an intellectual exercise (so from line 8 on) and the exercising of a more direct experiential encounter with the self. This experiential factor becomes especially pronounced at the level beyond intellect,

οὐ μέγεθός τι, ἀλλὰ περὶ ψυχήν, ἀχρώματον μὲν αὐτήν,   10
ἀχρώματον δὲ καὶ τὴν σωφροσύνην ἔχουσαν καὶ τὸ ἄλλο τῶν
ἀρετῶν φέγγος, ὅταν ἢ ἐν αὐτοῖς ἴδητε, ἢ καὶ ἐν ἄλλῳ
θεάσησθε μέγεθος ψυχῆς καὶ ἦθος δίκαιον καὶ σωφροσύνην
καθαρὰν καὶ ἀνδρίαν βλοσυρὸν ἔχουσαν πρόσωπον καὶ
σεμνότητα καὶ αἰδῶ ἐπιθέουσαν ἐν ἀτρεμεῖ καὶ ἀκύμονι καὶ   15
ἀπαθεῖ διαθέσει, ἐπὶ πᾶσι δὲ τούτοις τὸν θεοειδῆ νοῦν ἐπι-
λάμποντα. Ταῦτα οὖν ἀγάμενοι καὶ φιλοῦντες πῶς αὐτὰ
λέγομεν καλά; Ἔστι μὲν γὰρ καὶ φαίνεται καὶ οὐ μήποτε
ὁ ἰδὼν ἄλλο τι φῇ ἢ τὰ ὄντως ὄντα ταῦτα εἶναι. Τί
ὄντα ὄντως; Ἢ καλά. Ἀλλ' ἔτι ποθεῖ ὁ λόγος, τί ὄντα   20
πεποίηκε τὴν ψυχὴν εἶναι ἐράσμιον· τί τὸ ἐπὶ πάσαις

---

when the soul experiences the One, but can express this verbally or in
rational terms only in a way that captures the original experience in image
form. See especially 6.7.18–20, 6.9.3–5, and Smith 1992, VI.21–30.

5,10. ἀχρώματον: Plotinus is thinking here of *Phaedr.* 247c6, where Plato
speaks of a transcendent world of being that is without color or shape
(ἀχρώματός τε καὶ ἀσχημάτιστος καὶ ἀναφὴς οὐσία ὄντως οὖσα).

5,13–14. Our search "ascends" from soul (μέγεθος ψυχῆς, 5,10) to intellect (τὸν θεοειδῆ νοῦν, 5,16). In 6.1.1–4 he explains how we can reach our
own soul and eventually our intellect through the exercise of philosophical
introspection.

5,18. ἔστι μὲν γὰρ καὶ φαίνεται: "because they exist and are made manifest."

οὐ μήποτε with the subjunctive (or future indicative) to express a strong
denial.

5,19–21. ἤ here, as so often in Plotinus, expresses a strong affirmative
response. The virtual identity of Beauty with Being, first introduced here,
is a central idea of the treatise. For Plato Beauty is one Form among
others, whereas for Plotinus Beauty has an overriding function of char-
acterizing all Forms as Forms or archetypes of intelligible order. In this
way it has the same function as Being, which assures the reality of all
Forms and their unity as a coherent transcendent entity that is, for this

ἀρεταῖς διαπρέπον οἷον φῶς; Βούλει δὴ καὶ τὰ ἐναντία
λαβών, τὰ περὶ ψυχὴν αἰσχρὰ γινόμενα, ἀντιπαραθεῖναι;
Τάχα γὰρ ἂν συμβάλλοιτο πρὸς ὃ ζητοῦμεν τὸ αἰσχρὸν ὃ
τί ποτέ ἐστι καὶ διότι φανέν. Ἔστω δὴ ψυχὴ αἰσχρά,   25
ἀκόλαστός τε καὶ ἄδικος, πλείστων μὲν ἐπιθυμιῶν γέμουσα,
πλείστης δὲ ταραχῆς, ἐν φόβοις διὰ δειλίαν, ἐν φθόνοις

---

reason, able to impart to matter the coherence that we observe in the
physical world.

λόγος: "our enquiry" or "reason."

τί ὄντα ... ἐράσμιον: "Why (in what respect) has real being made the soul
loveable?" Note the introduction again of "love" as a motivating force in
the return to true being.

5,22. διαπρέπειν: "be preeminent" or "conspicuous," a word found mostly
in poetic contexts.

οἷον φῶς. Plotinus frequently uses the image of light to express the causal
effect or external activity of realities on what lies below them, as is implied
here with the suggestion that there is some higher cause that casts light
over the virtues, that is, accounts for their beauty. The ultimate source of
this image is Plato's analogy of the sun in *Resp.* 507b–509c. But although
usually employed as an analogy, Plotinus often understands this as more
than an analogy by identifying light with causal activity (e.g., 6.7.16,21–31;
5.3.8,19–25), so that we have a kind of "metaphysical" light that is akin
to, but not identical with, the incorporeal light that illuminates the physical world. With this concept he could emphasize the continuity of causal
activity from the One downward. It is an idea that was influential in Christian theology. See further Beierwaltes 1961 and Smith 2011, 13–19, with
the comments of Gurtler at Smith 2011, 23–26.

5,24–25. The entire phrase τὸ αἰσχρὸν ... φανέν forms the subject of
συμβάλλοιτο. "Clarity about the nature and cause of ugliness [lit. 'ugliness
having been made clear what it is and why'] would perhaps help us to find
what we are looking for."

διὰ μικροπρέπειαν, πάντα φρονοῦσα ἃ δὴ καὶ φρονεῖ θνητὰ
καὶ ταπεινά, σκολιὰ πανταχοῦ, ἡδονῶν οὐ καθαρῶν φίλη,
ζῶσα ζωὴν τοῦ ὅ τι ἂν πάθῃ διὰ σώματος ὡς ἡδὺ λαβοῦσα   30
αἶσχος. Αὐτὸ τοῦτο τὸ αἶσχος αὐτῇ ἄρα οὐ προσγε-
γονέναι οἷον ἐπακτὸν καλὸν φήσομεν, ὃ ἐλωβήσατο μὲν
αὐτῇ, πεποίηκε δὲ αὐτὴν ἀκάθαρτον καὶ πολλῷ τῷ κακῷ
συμπεφυρμένην, οὐδὲ ζωὴν ἔτι ἔχουσαν οὐδὲ αἴσθησιν
καθαράν, ἀλλὰ τῷ μίγματι τοῦ κακοῦ ἀμυδρᾷ τῇ ζωῇ   35
κεχρημένην καὶ πολλῷ τῷ θανάτῳ κεκραμένην, οὐκέτι μὲν
ὁρῶσαν ἃ δεῖ ψυχὴν ὁρᾶν, οὐκέτι δὲ ἐωμένην ἐν αὐτῇ
μένειν τῷ ἕλκεσθαι ἀεὶ πρὸς τὸ ἔξω καὶ τὸ κάτω καὶ τὸ
σκοτεινόν; Ἀκάθαρτος δή, οἶμαι, οὖσα καὶ φερομένη πανταχοῦ ὁλκαῖς πρὸς τὰ τῇ αἰσθήσει προσπίπτοντα, πολὺ τὸ   40
τοῦ σώματος ἔχουσα ἐγκεκραμένον, τῷ ὑλικῷ πολλῷ

5,28. μικροπρέπεια: "meanness." Cf. Aristotle, *Eth. nic.* 1107b20.

5,30. Literally "living a life consisting of [τοῦ, genitive dependent ζωὴν] whatever it experiences through the body, taking ugliness as delight," that is, "living a life of pure bodily sensations, taking ugliness as a delight."

5,32. οἷον ἐπακτὸν καλόν. The person with an "ugly" soul regards, in a perverted way, its "ugliness" to be beauty; in moral terms, what is evil would be seen as good. It is "brought in from outside" because beauty is intrinsic to the soul but may be obscured by evil that originates outside the soul. For the external origin of passions and evil in the soul, see 4.7.10,7–13.

5,33–34. πολλῷ τῷ κακῷ συμπεφυρμένην recalls Plato, *Phaed.* 66b5 (συμπεφυρμένη ᾖ ἡμῶν ἡ ψυχὴ μετὰ τοιούτου κακοῦ) and the ideas expressed there about the ways that our soul is impeded by the body.

5,39–50. We should not take these lines as applying to the limitations occasioned by mere physical embodiment but rather to the surrender to bodily temptations and material excess that are a feature of moral depravity. So the "mingling and inclination toward body and matter" (48–49) are to be interpreted as implying moral leaning or excessive involvement, which is clear from the reference to "overfamiliarity" (ἄγαν προσωμίλει, 5,55).

συνοῦσα καὶ εἰς αὐτὴν εἰσδεξαμένη εἶδος ἕτερον ἠλλάξατο
κράσει τῇ πρὸς τὸ χεῖρον· οἷον εἴ τις δὺς εἰς πηλὸν ἢ
βόρβορον τὸ μὲν ὅπερ εἶχε κάλλος μηκέτι προφαίνοι, τοῦτο
δὲ ὁρῷτο, ὃ παρὰ τοῦ πηλοῦ ἢ βορβόρου ἀπεμάξατο· ᾧ δὴ　　　45
τὸ αἰσχρὸν προσθήκῃ τοῦ ἀλλοτρίου προσῆλθε καὶ ἔργον
αὐτῷ, εἴπερ ἔσται πάλιν καλός, ἀπονιψαμένῳ καὶ καθηρα-
μένῳ ὅπερ ἦν εἶναι. Αἰσχρὰν δὴ ψυχὴν λέγοντες μίξει καὶ
κράσει καὶ νεύσει τῇ πρὸς τὸ σῶμα καὶ ὕλην ὀρθῶς ἂν
λέγοιμεν. Καὶ ἔστι τοῦτο αἶσχος ψυχῇ μὴ καθαρᾷ μηδὲ　　　50
εἰλικρινεῖ εἶναι ὥσπερ χρυσῷ, ἀναπεπλῆσθαι δὲ τοῦ
γεώδους, ὃ εἴ τις ἀφέλοι, καταλέλειπται χρυσὸς καὶ ἔστι
καλός, μονούμενος μὲν τῶν ἄλλων, αὑτῷ δὲ συνὼν μόνῳ.
Τὸν αὐτὸν δὴ τρόπον καὶ ψυχή, μονωθεῖσα μὲν ἐπιθυμιῶν,
ἃς διὰ τὸ σῶμα ἔχει, ᾧ ἄγαν προσωμίλει, ἀπαλλαγεῖσα δὲ　　　55
τῶν ἄλλων παθῶν καὶ καθαρθεῖσα ἃ ἔχει σωματωθεῖσα,

5,42. εἶδος. The word is to be understood in a general sense. There is no question of soul taking on a Form of ugliness.

ἠλλάξατο. Strictly speaking, of course, the soul is impassible and cannot change, but allowance must be made for moral "change." Sometimes, as here, the word ἀλλοίωσις (and its cognates) as opposed to κίνησις is used to express this. More generally, moral progression and failure are interpreted by the soul acting or failing to act in accordance with reason and the soul's own nature (see 3.6.1–6).

5,43. κράσει τῇ πρὸς τὸ χεῖρον. Supply ἑλκούσῃ τὴν ψυχήν, "a mixture that has made it worse." Cf. 5,49: κράσει καὶ νεύσει τῇ πρὸς τὸ σῶμα.

5,45. "what he has smeared onto himself from the mud and filth."

5,46. καὶ ἔργον αὐτῷ … . εἶναι. Supply ἐστί, so "his task is to be what he was before." In these lines Plotinus may be recalling passages from Plato's *Phaedo*, such as 69c1–6 (cf. Heraclitus DK B13.9–10) and 110a5–6 (πηλὸς ἀμήχανος καὶ βόρβοροι), in his description of this earth as opposed to the true heaven and earth. He may also have in mind the encrusted sea god Glaucus in Plato, *Resp.* 611d.

μείνασα μόνη τὸ αἰσχρὸν τὸ παρὰ τῆς ἑτέρας φύσεως
ἅπαν ἀπεθήκατο.

5,57. μόνη does not imply total isolation from all other souls or beings but rather being cut off from all that is inferior or impedes the realization of the true self. See on 6,11.

τῆς ἑτέρας φύσεως refers to matter. See 1.8.13,19 for the same phrase, which expresses the profound otherness of matter from all else.

5,58. ἀπεθήκατο: first aorist middle of ἀποτίθημι rather than the more usual second aorist ἀπέθετο.

Chapter 6

After we have identified physical beauty, we must then separate our souls from all that is material, a process analogous to religious "purification." When soul is separated from body in this sense (i.e., morally rather than by the physical separation that comes with death), it will be found to be not only beautiful but also the source of beauty. But the next stage, the discovery of our intellect, will bring us to an even greater level of beauty, where beauty is identical with being.

Having traced the ascent of the soul to the beautiful, Plotinus then (6,24–25) changes direction to follow the impact of beauty on the descending levels of reality, beginning with the One, through Intellect, the Soul, and finally the effect of the soul on body. The lowest point thus reached is then picked up at the beginning of the next chapter, where we are encouraged to begin our ascent "once more": ἀναβατέον οὖν πάλιν ἐπὶ τὸ ἀγαθόν.

6. Ἔστι γὰρ δή, ὡς ὁ παλαιὸς λόγος, καὶ ἡ σωφροσύνη
καὶ ἡ ἀνδρία καὶ πᾶσα ἀρετὴ κάθαρσις καὶ ἡ φρόνησις αὐτή. Διὸ καὶ αἱ τελεταὶ ὀρθῶς αἰνίττονται
τὸν μὴ κεκαθαρμένον καὶ εἰς Ἅιδου κείσεσθαι ἐν βορβόρῳ, ὅτι τὸ μὴ καθαρὸν βορβόρῳ διὰ κάκην φίλον· οἷα δὴ   5
καὶ ὕες, οὐ καθαραὶ τὸ σῶμα, χαίρουσι τῷ τοιούτῳ. Τί
γὰρ ἂν καὶ εἴη σωφροσύνη ἀληθὴς ἢ τὸ μὴ προσομιλεῖν ἡδο-
ναῖς τοῦ σώματος, φεύγειν δὲ ὡς οὐ καθαρὰς οὐδὲ καθαροῦ;
Ἡ δὲ ἀνδρία ἀφοβία θανάτου. Ὁ δέ ἐστιν ὁ θάνατος χωρὶς
εἶναι τὴν ψυχὴν τοῦ σώματος. Οὐ φοβεῖται δὲ τοῦτο, ὃς   10
ἀγαπᾷ μόνος γενέσθαι. Μεγαλοψυχία δὲ δὴ ὑπεροψία τῶν τῇ-

6,1. ὁ παλαιὸς λόγος. Plotinus often appeals in this way to the philosophical tradition up to the time of Aristotle and, more particularly, to the Presocratics and Plato (e.g., 2.9.10,13; 5.1.8,13). Here he probably has in mind Plato, *Phaed.* 69c, which has an Orphic background.

6,2–3. A long tradition going back beyond Plato identifies σωφροσύνη, ἀνδρία, δικαιοσύνη, and σοφία/φρόνησις as the four main virtues. Justice is omitted here but included with the other three in Plotinus's treatise *On Virtue* (1.2.). The prominence of φρόνησις (καὶ ἡ φρόνησις αὐτή) may indicate its special position with respect to the other virtues, an emphasis that goes back to Plato (Socrates) and was developed by the Stoics, for whom wisdom is the supreme, and indeed sole, virtue in that it embraces all the others.

For the description of the virtues as purifications, see Plato, *Phaed.* 69b–c; *Enn.* 1.2.3–4.

6,6. ὕες. An idea perhaps suggested by Plato, *Resp.* 535e4–5 (ὥσπερ θηρίον ὕειον) and Heraclitus DK B13 (ὕες βορβόρῳ ἥδονται μᾶλλον ἢ καθαρῷ ὕδατι).

6,9. ὁ δέ ἐστιν ὁ θάνατος: "and this is what death is, the separation...," a reminiscence, perhaps, of Plato's phraseology (*Phaed.* 64c5): καὶ εἶναι τοῦτον τὸ τεθνάναι, χωρίς.

6,11. μόνος. This does not refer to living a solitary life but rather to the life of freedom from dependence on external factors. See also 7,9.

δε. Ἡ δὲ φρόνησις νόησις ἐν ἀποστροφῇ τῶν κάτω, πρὸς δὲ
τὰ ἄνω τὴν ψυχὴν ἄγουσα. Γίνεται οὖν ἡ ψυχὴ καθαρθεῖσα

For μεγαλοψυχία, see Aristotle, *Eth. nic.* 1107b23.

6,13–24. Plotinus's line of thought here is not easy to follow. He opens with
a statement about the nature of soul in its purest state when it is most fully
itself. Since this state is dependent on its being turned toward intellect, he
explains what the soul receives from intellect, which is the source to the
soul of beauty and the rest of the forms. What soul receives is not alien to
its nature because it is in fact truly itself only when it is receptive of intellect. He can also conclude from this (6,18–19: διὸ καὶ λέγεται ὀρθῶς) that
this perfection of the soul as beautiful and good is to be identified with
ὁμοίωσις τῷ θεῷ. He now goes further (6,21: μᾶλλον δὲ...) to identify beauty
in the fullest sense (καλλονή) with real being, and finally (with a reference
back to chapter 5: the search for beauty by contrasting it with ugliness) he
draws the further conclusion (6,23: ὥστε ... καὶ) that καλλονή and goodness coincide in God (ἐκείνῳ in 6,23; see note on 6,23 as the interpretation
of this as the One).

6,13. γίνεται. The idea of moving from one status to another expressed by
γίνεται occurs frequently in Plotinus. In this treatise we may refer to 9,15
and 31–32, where he seems to suggest that we "become" intellect. In the
present chapter he does not go this far but holds the individual within the
limits of soul. The transition of the individual from one discrete level of
reality to another is more clearly asserted in 5.3.4,10–13, where we are said
to "become intellect" (ἐκεῖνον γινόμενον ... ἄλλον γενόμενον); that is, there
is a transition within the levels of the self. What moves is less clear: a sort
of floating self or focal point that determines the level at which our real
lives are conducted. This floating self is not easily accommodated within
the structure of traditional Greek metaphysical thought, and this is at least
one of the reasons why later Neoplatonists were highly critical of Plotinus's concept of an undescended part of the soul. For the undescended
part of the soul, see 4.8.8,1–3; for the way in which this might be linked
with a floating self, see 5.3.4,13–15: "and by that Intellect he thinks himself
again, not any longer as man, but having become altogether other and
snatching himself up to the higher world, *drawing up only the better part
of soul*, which alone is able to be winged for intellection, *by which someone*

εἶδος καὶ λόγος καὶ πάντη ἀσώματος καὶ νοερὰ καὶ ὅλη τοῦ
θείου, ὅθεν ἡ πηγὴ τοῦ καλοῦ καὶ τὰ συγγενῆ πάντα   15
τοιαῦτα. Ψυχὴ οὖν ἀναχθεῖσα πρὸς νοῦν ἐπὶ τὸ μᾶλλόν ἐστι
καλόν. Νοῦς δὲ καὶ τὰ παρὰ νοῦ τὸ κάλλος αὐτῇ οἰκεῖον
καὶ οὐκ ἀλλότριον, ὅτι τότε ἐστὶν ὄντως μόνον ψυχή. Διὸ
καὶ λέγεται ὀρθῶς τὸ ἀγαθὸν καὶ καλὸν τὴν ψυχὴν γίνεσθαι

---

in the intelligible may store up for himself what he saw [in the intelligible]."
The concluding phrase, ἵνα τις ἐκεῖ παρακαταθοῖτο ἃ εἶδε, seems to refer to
the way in which our ordinary consciousness can somehow possess some
awareness of what is contemplated at the level of our intellect.

6,14–15. ὅλη τοῦ θείου. Plotinus ascribes divinity to transcendent reality in
a flexible manner; both the soul and intellect may be described as divine.

6,15. ὅθεν. From the divine, that is, Intellect.

6,15–16. τὰ συγγενῆ πάντα τοιαῦτα: "all the kind of things related to it," that
is, the Forms and virtues.

6,16. ἐπί. LSJ, s.v. "ἐπί," III.2 "with respect to." Cf. 2.3.12,19: ἐπὶ τὸ μᾶλλόν
καὶ ἧττον θερμά.

6,17. καλόν (neuter) "agrees" with ψυχὴ. Similarly in line 19, where τὸ is to
be taken with γίνεσθαι. For this usage of the neuter, common in philosophy, see the introduction above, p. 18.

6,18. τότε. When the soul is turned toward intellect.

6,19. We note here the unexpected introduction of what is ἀγαθός along-
side beauty. It serves in the exposition to link beauty with the Good (the
One), which is beyond Intellect and being, and reminds us that for Plotinus moral and aesthetic values are intertwined. The same purpose is
served by explicitly defining matter (ugliness) as the "primary evil." The
next chapter then takes up this theme where it begins with our ascent "to
the Good." In fact, the treatise as a whole is gradually extending its range
of vision from beauty alone to the broader values subsumed under beauty

ὁμοιωθῆναι εἶναι θεῷ, ὅτι ἐκεῖθεν τὸ καλὸν καὶ ἡ μοῖρα ἡ 20
ἑτέρα τῶν ὄντων. Μᾶλλον δὲ τὰ ὄντα ἡ καλλονή ἐστιν, ἡ
δ' ἑτέρα φύσις τὸ αἰσχρόν, τὸ δ' αὐτὸ καὶ πρῶτον κακόν,
ὥστε κἀκείνῳ ταὐτὸν ἀγαθόν τε καὶ καλόν, ἢ τἀγαθόν

---

in the transcendent world and their concomitant expressions in our moral stance in this world.

6,20. ὁμοιωθῆναι εἶναι θεῷ. To make ourselves like god became established as the primary aim of the Platonist, the formula being taken from Plato, *Theaet.* 176b. See Sedley 1997 and 1999. In the formula here, "god," who is the source of beauty, is to be identified with Intellect (rather than with the One), since the following sentence, in making the strong assertion that being (i.e., the Intelligible realm) is not only the cause of beauty but is identical with it, implies that the "god" to whose likeness we must aspire is Intellect.

ἐκεῖθεν. From god who is νοῦς.

6,20–21. ἡ μοῖρα ἡ ἑτέρα τῶν ὄντων. This is a probable reminiscence of θείας ... μοίρας (Plato, *Phaedr.* 230a5–6); cf. 4.2.1,5: τῆς θείας μοίρας εἶναι (sc.τὴν ψυχὴν). ὄντων is not a partitive genitive but a genitive of description: "the divine part that consists of real being" and that is "other than" that which is ugly.

6,21. μᾶλλον δὲ τὰ ὄντα ἡ καλλονή ἐστιν. This "corrective" (μᾶλλον) statement goes beyond what has so far been maintained, that "beauty" is found in the soul, although it has its source above soul in Intellect. Now Plotinus claims that beauty is identical with Being (Intellect).
καλλονή is a rare word, used by Plato (*Symp.* 206d2) and by Plotinus only here and in 6.2.18,1 and 6.7.33,22, where it is ascribed to the One.

6,22. ἡ ἑτέρα φύσις is matter.

6,23. κἀκείνῳ: god. But does Plotinus mean Intellect, as in the preceding lines, or has he now, in a supplementary conclusion (ὥστε καὶ ἐκείνῳ; see note on 6,13–24), introduced the One? The following lines, which clearly

τε καὶ καλλονή. Ὁμοίως οὖν ζητητέον καλόν τε καὶ
ἀγαθὸν καὶ αἰσχρόν τε καὶ κακόν. Καὶ τὸ πρῶτον θετέον   25
τὴν καλλονήν, ὅπερ καὶ τἀγαθόν· ἀφ' οὗ νοῦς εὐθὺς τὸ

---

identify the One with καλλονή and τὸ ἀγαθόν, support the latter interpretation.

6,24–25. The argument is a little obscure here, primarily because Plotinus is making a transition from Intellect to the One. This is partly done by introducing the idea that soul and *nous* are not only καλά but also ἀγαθά, and the One is elsewhere identified by Plotinus with τὸ ἀγαθόν, Plato's ultimate principle in *Resp.* 6. Is beauty, then, also found at its highest level in the One? This is an issue about which Plotinus sometimes wavers (see the discussion on the last lines of this treatise). But here at least he affirms strongly (6,25–27) that καλλονή is identical with τὸ ἀγαθόν and the One. Indeed, the very use at 6,21 of the unusual word καλλονή, which we have noted is elsewhere applied by him only to the One, aids the transition to the higher level.

6,24. ὁμοίως ("in a similar way") refers to the analysis in the preceding section, which sharply distinguishes all that is beautiful from what is ugly. What is new about the next stage of the enquiry is that it seeks to derive beauty, as it is manifested at each level of reality, by beginning with its ultimate cause and tracing its effect from the highest principle downward rather than as before from the physical world upward.

6,25–26. Note the different expressions used to convey the sequence of levels:

the One	ἡ καλλονή	beautifulness
νοῦς	τὸ καλόν	the beautiful
ψυχή	νῷ καλόν	beautiful (caused by νοῦς)
this world	παρὰ ψυχῆς μορφούσης καλά	beautiful by participation in soul

καλόν· ψυχὴ δὲ νῷ καλόν· τὰ δὲ ἄλλα ἤδη παρὰ ψυχῆς
μορφούσης καλά, τά τε ἐν ταῖς πράξεσι τά τε ἐν τοῖς
ἐπιτηδεύμασι. Καὶ δὴ καὶ τὰ σώματα, ὅσα οὕτω λέγεται,
ψυχὴ ἤδη ποιεῖ· ἅτε γὰρ θεῖον οὖσα καὶ οἷον μοῖρα τοῦ   30
καλοῦ, ὧν ἂν ἐφάψηται καὶ κρατῇ, καλὰ ταῦτα, ὡς δυνατὸν
αὐτοῖς μεταλαβεῖν, ποιεῖ.

6,31–32. ὡς δυνατὸν αὐτοῖς μεταλαβεῖν. Plotinus has two solutions to the
question why matter does not always reflect all aspects or degrees of form.
(1) The recipient is not able to receive everything; this presents difficulties,
if we are speaking of prime matter, since it would ascribe to it the "positive"
property of not being able to receive or being able to restrict certain forms.
(2) The power of form, each successive level of which is seen as a λόγος
or image of its prior, becomes progressively weaker. In this way Plotinus
can, for example, account (6.7.9) for the fact that a horse, which does not
possess reason, may have as its ultimate cause a form or intelligible reality
that by definition must have reason (intellect): "for as the powers unfold
they always leave something behind on a higher level (ἐξελιττόμεναι γὰρ αἱ
δυνάμεις καταλείπουσιν ἀεὶ εἰς τὸ ἄνω, 6.7.9,38–39).

Chapter 7

After establishing more clearly the metaphysical framework within which the individual makes his or her ascent to Intellect and the One, Plotinus now calls on us again (πάλιν), in more practical terms, to make the ascent to true beauty and describes what our search for it implies for the way in which we conduct our earthly lives. He also emphasizes both the basic human urge toward the Good and the impact on us of the personal experience of encountering beauty. Both of these are expressed in powerful metaphorical language, much of it borrowed from Plato's *Symposium*, *Timaeus*, and *Phaedrus*. In the concluding lines (7,30–39) the more extensive significance of the search for beauty and the ultimate purpose of the treatise is explicitly revealed, for the search for true beauty is extended beyond transcending physical beauty to include the rejection, too, of all other physical and external goods. This vision is based on the coincidence of true beauty and goodness and the identification of true beauty with intelligible reality in its entirety. The search for true beauty will then lead to moral and spiritual perfection.

7. Ἀναβατέον οὖν πάλιν ἐπὶ τὸ ἀγαθόν, οὗ ὀρέγεται
πᾶσα ψυχή. Εἴ τις οὖν εἶδεν αὐτό, οἶδεν ὃ λέγω, ὅπως
καλόν. Ἐφετὸν μὲν γὰρ ὡς ἀγαθὸν καὶ ἡ ἔφεσις πρὸς
τοῦτο, τεῦξις δὲ αὐτοῦ ἀναβαίνουσι πρὸς τὸ ἄνω καὶ
ἐπιστραφεῖσι καὶ ἀποδυομένοις ἃ καταβαίνοντες ἠμφιέσ-
μεθα· οἷον ἐπὶ τὰ ἅγια τῶν ἱερῶν τοῖς ἀνιοῦσι καθάρσεις

5

7,1–2. οὗ ὀρέγεται πᾶσα ψυχή. The innate desire for the Good in both the human soul and the tendency of all that exists to seek its perfection in the Good is based ultimately on Plato's insight about the power of "love" in the *Symposium*. For Plotinus, it is represented by the inbuilt force that causes all hypostases to cease their outward movement (procession) from their producers and to return upon them in contemplation, thus perfecting their own natures. This is seen most crucially in the very first product of the One, Intellect, whose procession (and return) is described in 5.2.1,7– 14: "the One, perfect because it seeks nothing, has nothing, and needs nothing, overflows, as it were, and its superabundance makes something other than itself. This, when it has come into being, turns back upon the One and is filled and becomes Intellect by looking toward it. Its halt and turning toward the One constitute being, its gaze upon the One Intellect. Since it halts and turns toward the One that it may see, it becomes simultaneously Intellect and being" (trans. Armstrong, adapted). The human soul strives in the same way to participate in this universal dynamic of procession and return, but without the permanence and timelessness of completely transcendent realities.

7,2. εἴ τις οὖν εἶδεν αὐτό. This appeal to personal experience is important for Plotinus. We learn from 6.9 (see especially 6.9.11) that personal experience of the One, for example, is an important adjunct to discursive arguments that point to it. On this topic, see Smith 1992.

7,4. ἀναβαίνουσι. Dative plural of the participle meaning "for those making the ascent."

7,6. τοῖς ἀνιοῦσι. The reference here to religious ritual recalls the allusion to mystery rites in the previous chapter and helps to provide thematic coherence, although a different aspect (that of divesting oneself of garments) is described.

τε καὶ ἱματίων ἀποθέσεις τῶν πρὶν καὶ τὸ γυμνοῖς ἀνιέναι·
ἕως ἄν τις παρελθὼν ἐν τῇ ἀναβάσει πᾶν ὅσον ἀλλότριον
τοῦ θεοῦ αὐτῷ μόνῳ αὐτὸ μόνον ἴδῃ εἰλικρινές, ἁπλοῦν,

The initial phrase, ἀποδυομένοις ἃ καταβαίνοντες ἠμφιέσμεθα (7,5–6: "divested themselves of the garments they put on in their descent"), is syntactically not part of the ritual metaphor, which is introduced with οἷον, and must therefore refer to a nonmetaphorical process: the idea that the soul, in its descent through the planetary spheres, takes on different faculties like garments. This idea, which was a commonplace, may be found in Porphyry (*Sent.* 29) and would have been familiar to Plotinus's students. Although Plotinus was not generally interested in contemporary religious practice, he does occasionally, as here, make direct and noncritical allusion to it. His employment of such ideas as metaphor, as in the rest of this passage, is more common and unproblematic (and is found in Plato, too, e.g., *Phaedr.* 250b8 and e1). But the direct allusion to nonphilosophical ideas has been a source of concern to some interpreters anxious to defend Plotinus's reputation as a "rational" thinker and has led them to neglect or even dismiss them. It is true that Plotinus was less inclined than most of his contemporaries to such ideas; one notes, for example, the clear bafflement of Porphyry (*Vit. Plot.* 10,37–38) and his fellow students at Plotinus's declaration, when requested to visit some temples with them, that "the gods should come to him, not he to them." But it is clear that he could also be sympathetic to the interest of his contemporaries in religious ideas and practices. One may cite, for example, his praise of Porphyry as philosopher and hierophant (*Vit. Plot.* 15,5), the exploitation of myth (and Platonic myth) in 3.5, and his acceptance of the traditional doctrine of the transmigration of souls expressed in a literal rather than a metaphorical sense.

7,8. παρελθὼν. The prefix has the force of "transcending, passing beyond."

7,9. αὐτῷ μόνῳ αὐτὸ μόνον. Compare 6.9.11,51 (φυγὴ μόνου πρὸς μόνον), which also describes the very highest level of "aloneness," the union with the One that is the ultimate alone. The meaning of personal aloneness is of separation from all that is external and less than the inner self. It does not, however, exclude other "selves," since at this level all selves are in a sense one.

καθαρόν, ἀφ' οὗ πάντα ἐξήρτηται καὶ πρὸς αὐτὸ βλέπει   10
καὶ ἔστι καὶ ζῇ καὶ νοεῖ· ζωῆς γὰρ αἴτιος καὶ νοῦ καὶ τοῦ
εἶναι. Τοῦτο οὖν εἴ τις ἴδοι, ποίους ἂν ἴσχοι ἔρωτας,
ποίους δὲ πόθους, βουλόμενος αὐτῷ συγκερασθῆναι, πῶς
δ' ἂν ἐκπλαγείη μεθ' ἡδονῆς; Ἔστι γὰρ τῷ μὲν μήπω ἰδόντι
ὀρέγεσθαι ὡς ἀγαθοῦ· τῷ δὲ ἰδόντι ὑπάρχει ἐπὶ καλῷ   15
ἀγασθαί τε καὶ θάμβους πίμπλασθαι μεθ' ἡδονῆς καὶ ἐκπλήττεσθαι ἀβλαβῶς καὶ ἐρᾶν ἀληθῆ ἔρωτα καὶ δριμεῖς πόθους καὶ τῶν ἄλλων ἐρώτων καταγελᾶν καὶ τῶν πρόσθεν νομιζομένων καλῶν καταφρονεῖν· ὁποῖον πάσχουσιν ὅσοι θεῶν εἴ-

---

7,9–10. εἰλικρινές ... καθαρόν. See Plato, *Symp.* 211e1.

7,10–11. These lines express in brief form important metaphysical principles. The notion of procession and return may be seen in ἐξήρτηται
(the causal dependence of a lower principle from a higher from which it
proceeds) and πρὸς αὐτὸ βλέπει (the contemplation of the higher by the
lower—its return). For Plotinus each level of reality (the One, Intellect,
and Soul) acts as both cause and goal, as efficient and final cause, to what
is below it, which is only then fully constituted when it turns back in contemplation of its prior. The following phrase echoes the constituent aspects
of the intelligible world, ὄν, ζωή, νοῦς, which were to become a formulaic
"triad" for later Neoplatonists (see Hadot 1957).

7,12–14. Note the tricolon: ποίους ... ποίους ... πῶς....

7,14. ἐκπλαγείη. There is no need to add a negative with HS4.

7,15. ὀρέγεσθαι. As with ὀρέγεται at the beginning of the chapter, this
expresses the basic human urge toward beauty and the Good.

7,16–17. ἐκπλήττεσθαι. In *Phaedr.* 250a6 ἐκπλήττονται describes the experience that souls have of true beauty. The very physical language used by
Plotinus for this experience is inspired largely by Plato.

7,18–19. τῶν πρόσθεν νομιζομένων καλῶν καταφρονεῖν. This apparently
strong rejection of physical beauty must be seen in context. Elsewhere
it is clear that Plotinus values physical beauty in itself (see the introduc-

δεσιν ἢ δαιμόνων προστυχόντες οὐκέτ᾽ ἂν ἀποδέχοιντο ὁμοίως   20
ἄλλων κάλλη σωμάτων. Τί δῆτα οἰόμεθα, εἴ τις αὐτὸ
τὸ καλὸν θεῷτο αὐτὸ ἐφ᾽ ἑαυτοῦ καθαρόν, μὴ σαρκῶν, μὴ σώματος ἀνάπλεων, μὴ ἐν γῇ, μὴ ἐν οὐρανῷ,
ἵν᾽ ᾖ καθαρόν; Καὶ γὰρ ἐπακτὰ πάντα ταῦτα καὶ μέμικται καὶ
οὐ πρῶτα, παρ᾽ ἐκείνου δέ. Εἰ οὖν ἐκεῖνο, ὃ χορηγεῖ μὲν   25
ἅπασιν, ἐφ᾽ ἑαυτοῦ δὲ μένον δίδωσι καὶ οὐ δέχεταί τι εἰς

tion above, pp. 13–15) but demotes it, as here, when compared with transcendent beauty. The same ambivalence applies to the material world as a
whole when compared with its intelligible archetype.

7,19–20. Plotinus is here drawing an analogy between the increased intensity people experience when beholding the beauty of the (visible) gods
compared with other beautiful physical bodies and the intense joy of
encountering intelligible compared with physical beauty. With the forms
of gods and daimones, Plotinus is probably thinking of the stars, which are
divine, and the theophanies of daimones and gods of the kind recounted
in *Vit. Plot.* 10.

7,20. ὁμοίως: "no longer … in the same way," that is, not with the same
intensity as people experience the manifestations of gods.

7,21–23. Cf. Plato, *Symp.* 211d8–e2: τί δῆτα, ἔφη, οἰόμεθα, εἴ τῳ γένοιτο
αὐτὸ τὸ καλὸν ἰδεῖν εἰλικρινές, καθαρόν, ἄμεικτον, ἀλλὰ μὴ ἀνάπλεων σαρκῶν
τε ἀνθρωπίνων καὶ χρωμάτων καὶ ἄλλης πολλῆς φλυαρίας θνητῆς…;

7,23. μὴ ἐν γῇ, μὴ ἐν οὐρανῷ refer respectively to ἄλλων σωμάτων (7,21) and
θεῶν εἴδεσιν ἢ δαιμόνων (7,19–20).

7,25. ἐκείνου: that is, αὐτὸ τὸ καλόν.

7,26. ἐφ᾽ ἑαυτοῦ δὲ μένον δίδωσι. A succinct reference to another basic
metaphysical principle, that transcendent realities produce and perfect
what is beneath them without being affected or diminished in any way.

αὐτό, ἴδοι, μένων ἐν τῇ θέᾳ τοῦ τοιούτου καὶ ἀπολαύων
αὐτοῦ ὁμοιούμενος, τίνος ἂν ἔτι δέοιτο καλοῦ; Τοῦτο γὰρ
αὐτὸ μάλιστα κάλλος ὂν αὐτὸ καὶ τὸ πρῶτον ἐργάζεται
τοὺς ἐραστὰς αὐτοῦ καλοὺς καὶ ἐραστοὺς ποιεῖ. Οὗ δὴ καὶ   30
ἀγὼν μέγιστος καὶ ἔσχατος ψυχαῖς πρόκειται, ὑπὲρ
οὗ καὶ ὁ πᾶς πόνος, μὴ ἀμοίρους γενέσθαι τῆς ἀρίστης θέας,
ἧς ὁ μὲν τυχὼν μακάριος ὄψιν μακαρίαν τεθεαμένος·
ἀτυχὴς δὲ [οὗτος] ὁ μὴ τυχών. Οὐ γὰρ ὁ χρωμάτων ἢ σωμάτων καλῶν μὴ τυχὼν οὐδὲ δυνάμεως οὐδὲ ἀρχῶν οὐδὲ ὁ   35
βασιλείας μὴ τυχὼν ἀτυχής, ἀλλ’ ὁ τούτου καὶ μόνου, ὑπὲρ

7,27. αὐτό here, as so often in Plotinus, for ἑαυτό. But it is sometimes difficult to decide whether forms with the smooth breathing have reflexive force.

εἰ οὖν ἐκεῖνο … ἴδοι (27): the subject of ἴδοι is τις referring back to line 21, and the object is ἐκεῖνο.

7,31–32. Cf. Plato, *Phaedr.* 247b5–6: ἔνθα δὴ πόνος τε καὶ ἀγὼν ἔσχατος ψυχῇ πρόκειται; and 250b6: μακαρίαν ὄψιν τε καὶ θέαν.

7,32. μὴ ἀμοίρους γενέσθαι. The infinitive is in apposition to πόνος.

7,36. τούτου καὶ μόνου: "of this and this alone." The genitive is dependent on μὴ τυχών: ὁ μὴ τυχὼν τούτου καὶ τούτου μόνου. Plotinus here suggests that external advantages need play no part in the pursuit of happiness, for true happiness may be attained solely by assimilation with god. The final clause (7,38: εἰ καταλιπών τις…, "so long as…"), however, restores some recognition of external goods: they should only be rejected if that will assist in realizing true happiness. The treatise 1.4 (46), written near the end of Plotinus's life, contains the most extreme statement of this doctrine, where he claims that the good person will be happy even in the bull of Phalaris (a stock example of extreme torture), for although the empirical self will be suffering (and in the conventional sense "not happy"), the internal contemplation of the one who has attained the higher level of life, one's true self or intellect, will remain undisturbed. But even in this treatise Plotinus still implies a role for external goods and activities, when at the end (1.4.16) he compares the body to a musical instrument that has been given for our use: "And the instrument was not given to him [the good

οὗ τῆς τεύξεως καὶ βασιλείας καὶ ἀρχὰς γῆς ἁπάσης καὶ
θαλάττης καὶ οὐρανοῦ προέσθαι χρεών, εἰ καταλιπών τις
ταῦτα καὶ ὑπεριδὼν εἰς ἐκεῖνο στραφεὶς ἴδοι.

---

man] in the first place to no purpose, for he has often made use of it up to
now." But external goods are, of course, always subordinate to, and never
supplant, the contemplative self-sufficiency of the truly good person.

7,36–37. ὑπὲρ οὗ τῆς τεύξεως. οὗ is objective genitive dependent on ὑπὲρ
τῆς τεύξεως: "for the attainment of which…."

Chapter 8

In a series of vivid images and allusions Plotinus exhorts us to "escape" from the world of lower beauty. The stress is on our own efforts to use the faculty of vision that we all possess.

8. Τίς οὖν ὁ τρόπος; Τίς μηχανή; Πῶς τις θεάσηται
κάλλος ἀμήχανον οἷον ἔνδον ἐν ἁγίοις ἱεροῖς μένον
οὐδὲ προϊὸν εἰς τὸ ἔξω, ἵνα τις καὶ βέβηλος ἴδη; Ἴτω δὴ
καὶ συνεπέσθω εἰς τὸ εἴσω ὁ δυνάμενος ἔξω καταλιπὼν ὄψιν
ὀμμάτων μηδ' ἐπιστρέφων αὐτὸν εἰς τὰς προτέρας ἀγλαΐας   5
σωμάτων. Ἰδόντα γὰρ δεῖ τὰ ἐν σώμασι καλὰ μήτοι
προστρέχειν, ἀλλὰ γνόντας ὥς εἰσιν εἰκόνες καὶ ἴχνη καὶ
σκιαὶ φεύγειν πρὸς ἐκεῖνο οὗ ταῦτα εἰκόνες. Εἰ γάρ τις
ἐπιδράμοι λαβεῖν βουλόμενος ὡς ἀληθινόν, οἷα εἰδώλου

8,1. Note the tricolon with the third member of increased length: τίς
... τίς ... πῶς.... In the opening two lines Plotinus playfully combines
two Platonic passages: *Phileb.* 16b7, where Protarchus begs Socrates to
tell him what τρόπος or μηχανή he would recommend to extract himself from the difficulties of the argument in which he finds himself; and
Resp. 509a6, where the Idea of the Good is compared with the sun and
is described as a κάλλος ἀμήχανον, exploiting the "paradox" afforded by
μηχανή/ἀμήχανον.

8,2–3. οἷον ... ἔξω. The sustained imagery of religious ritual strengthens
the continuity of this with the previous two chapters.

8,5. αὐτὸν with reflexive meaning.

8,7. προστρέχειν. We should supply an object: "rush up to them." The word
is found only here in Plotinus and is clearly pejorative. Could this be a
reminiscence of Plato, *Resp.* 440a2: προσδραμὼν πρὸς τοὺς νεκρούς?

8,8–9. The reference is to the myth of Narcissus, on which see Hadot 1976.
For the myth itself, see Ovid, *Metam.* 3.339–510; Pausanias, *Descr.* 9.31.7–
9; and Philostratus, *Imag.* 1.23. In Plotinus's version Narcissus does not die
but simply slips into the water after his image. He probably has the same
myth in mind in 5.8[31].2,34–35 (*On Intelligible Beauty*): "like someone
who sees his own image but does not know where it came from and chases
after it."

καλοῦ ἐφ᾽ ὕδατος ὀχουμένου, ὁ λαβεῖν βουληθείς, ὥς πού   10
τις μῦθος, δοκῶ μοι, αἰνίττεται, δὺς εἰς τὸ κάτω τοῦ
ῥεύματος ἀφανὴς ἐγένετο, τὸν αὐτὸν δὴ τρόπον ὁ ἐχόμενος
τῶν καλῶν σωμάτων καὶ μὴ ἀφιεὶς οὐ τῷ σώματι, τῇ δὲ
ψυχῇ καταδύσεται εἰς σκοτεινὰ καὶ ἀτερπῆ τῷ νῷ βάθη, ἔνθα
τυφλὸς ἐν Ἅιδου μένων καὶ ἐνταῦθα κἀκεῖ σκιαῖς συν-   15
έσται. Φεύγωμεν δὴ φίλην ἐς πατρίδα, ἀληθέστερον
ἄν τις παρακελεύοιτο. Τίς οὖν ἡ φυγὴ καὶ πῶς; Ἀναξόμεθα
οἷον ἀπὸ μάγου Κίρκης φησὶν ἢ Καλυψοῦς Ὀδυσσεὺς

8,10–11. The tentative way (που, δοκῶ μοι) in which Plotinus introduces his interpretation of this well-known myth suggests that it is original to him.

8,13. καὶ μὴ ἀφιεὶς ("and not letting go") is to be taken along with ἐχόμενος.

8,13–14. οὐ τῷ σώματι, τῇ δὲ ψυχῇ. These two contrasting phrases (οὐ … δὲ) are to be construed with καταδύσεται.

8,15. καὶ ἐνταῦθα κἀκεῖ. ἐνταῦθα and ἐκεῖ refer respectively to life in this world and in the next. Both are designated as Hades but in a metaphorical and a literal sense: Hades is a metaphorical way of describing the life in this world of the nonphilosopher who sees only images (shadows) of true reality; the real Hades is peopled by "shadows" (the shades of the dead). Plotinus thought that the soul of the philosopher would escape the real Hades, which would remain the location of unenlightened souls after their death.

8,16. The quotation is from Homer, *Il.* 2.140. As often, Plotinus ignores the context of the lines (it is uttered by the Greeks in their wish to abandon the siege of Troy and return home). But the phrase φίλην ἐς πατρίδα occurs frequently in the *Odyssey* (interpreted in general by the Neoplatonists as an allegory of the return of the soul to its heavenly home) and links the quotation more effectively into the context of the *Odyssey* references in the following lines.

8,18. The subject of φησίν is Homer. Understand ἀνήχθη with Ὀδυσσεὺς. See Homer, *Od.* 5.77–268 for Calypso and 10.133–574 for Circe. There was

αἰνιττόμενος, δοκεῖ μοι, μεῖναι οὐκ ἀρεσθείς, καίτοι ἔχων
ἡδονὰς δι' ὀμμάτων καὶ κάλλει πολλῷ αἰσθητῷ συνών.   20
Πατρὶς δὴ ἡμῖν, ὅθεν παρήλθομεν, καὶ πατὴρ ἐκεῖ. Τίς
οὖν ὁ στόλος καὶ ἡ φυγή; Οὐ ποσὶ δεῖ διανύσαι· πανταχοῦ
γὰρ φέρουσι πόδες ἐπὶ γῆν ἄλλην ἀπ' ἄλλης· οὐδέ σε δεῖ

---

in antiquity a long tradition of allegorizing Homer as here, for example, in
interpreting the journey of Odysseus as the return of the soul to its original home (see Lamberton 1989). Although Odysseus is not mentioned by
name, Plotinus probably has him in mind when describing the sort of man
who succeeds in reaching the intelligible world of the real self, as being
"like a man who arrives in his well-governed land after a long journey"
(5.9.1,20–21). Porphyry discourses on the nature of the souls of Odysseus's
men who had been transformed by Circe into animals (F.382 Smith), and,
in his *Cave of the Nymphs*, a discourse on the meaning of Homer, *Od.*
13.102–112, Odysseus's arrival at the harbor of Phorcys is interpreted as
symbolizing the end of the soul's journey (chs. 24–25). In the same passage
Porphyry expresses his general approval of Numenius's allegorization of
the *Odyssey*: "For it is my opinion that Numenius and his school were correct in thinking that for Homer in the *Odyssey*, Odysseus bears a symbol
of one who passes through the stages of genesis and, in doing so, returns
to those beyond every wave." For Calypso, see also the Nag Hammadi tractate *Exegesis of the Soul* (NHC II 6) 136.27–35.

8,21. πατήρ is often used by Plotinus of Intellect or the One, a usage that
probably reflects Homer's way of referring to Zeus and, more immediately,
Plato, *Tim.* 28c3 and 37c7, where the demiurge who creates the world is
called πατήρ. For Intellect, see *Enn.* 5.1.1,3 and the image of ourselves as
"children" separated from their fathers (1,9–10); see also 2.9.2,4 and 16,9;
for the One, see 5.8.1,3.

8,23. σε. Note the way in which the tone becomes more intimate in the
course of the exhortations in this chapter. It begins with the third-person (ἴτω), then moves with the quotation from Homer to the first-person
plural (ἀναξόμεθα, ἡμῖν, παρήλθομεν) before concluding with the second-
person singular (σε).

ἵππων ὄχημα ἤ τι θαλάττιον παρασκευάσαι, ἀλλὰ ταῦτα
πάντα ἀφεῖναι δεῖ καὶ μὴ βλέπειν, ἀλλ' οἷον μύσαντα ὄψιν   25
ἄλλην ἀλλάξασθαι καὶ ἀνεγεῖραι, ἣν ἔχει μὲν πᾶς, χρῶνται
δὲ ὀλίγοι.

8,25. μύσαντα (shutting the eyes) shares the same root as μυστήριον,
μυστικῶς, although Plotinus here is probably thinking primarily of the
physical metaphor of shutting the eyes. See Celsus (Origen, *Cels.* 7.39):
"Only then will you see god, if you shut your eyes to perceptions [αἰσθήσεσι
μύσαντες] and look up with your mind and, turning away the eye of flesh,
awaken the eye of the soul." The idea of linking improved inner vision
with diminished external vision also recalls Plato, *Symp.* 219a2–4: "A
man's mental vision does not begin to be keen until his physical vision is
past its prime."

8,26–27. Plotinus here affirms that the highest level of contemplation
is accessible for all people—there is no elite—even though few in fact
manage to attain it. This optimism is supported by his doctrine that part
of our soul remains undescended (see note on 6,13), thus providing us
with a link that we can use to reach the transcendent. Later Platonists
strongly rejected the notion of an undescended part of the soul and cor-
respondingly reduced the status of the human soul and its possibility of
reaching the Intelligible.

Chapter 9

The faculty of vision alluded to at the end of the previous chapter is now more fully explained by referring back to the idea of inner sight that is awakened by viewing external beauty, which in turn leads us to find true beauty both within external objects and within our own selves. When we have fully identified ourselves with the beauty within, we no longer need instruction or philosophical discourse to assimilate ourselves with the ultimate principle, the One. This naturally leads to the question whether Intellect or the One is to be identified with Beauty itself.

9. Τί οὖν ἐκείνη ἡ ἔνδον βλέπει; Ἄρτι μὲν ἐγειρομένη
οὐ πάνυ τὰ λαμπρὰ δύναται βλέπειν. Ἐθιστέον οὖν τὴν
ψυχὴν αὐτὴν πρῶτον μὲν τὰ καλὰ βλέπειν ἐπιτηδεύματα·
εἶτα ἔργα καλά, οὐχ ὅσα αἱ τέχναι ἐργάζονται, ἀλλ' ὅσα οἱ
ἄνδρες οἱ λεγόμενοι ἀγαθοί· εἶτα ψυχὴν ἴδε τῶν τὰ ἔργα τὰ   5
καλὰ ἐργαζομένων. Πῶς ἂν οὖν ἴδοις ψυχὴν ἀγαθὴν οἷον
τὸ κάλλος ἔχει; Ἄναγε ἐπὶ σαυτὸν καὶ ἴδε· κἂν μήπω
σαυτὸν ἴδῃς καλόν, οἷα ποιητὴς ἀγάλματος, ὃ δεῖ καλὸν
γενέσθαι, τὸ μὲν ἀφαιρεῖ, τὸ δὲ ἀπέξεσε, τὸ δὲ λεῖον, τὸ
δὲ καθαρὸν ἐποίησεν, ἕως ἔδειξε καλὸν ἐπὶ τῷ ἀγάλματι   10
πρόσωπον, οὕτω καὶ σὺ ἀφαίρει ὅσα περιττὰ καὶ ἀπεύθυνε

9,1. ἐκείνη ἡ ἔνδον. Understand ὄψις from 8,25.

9,2. οὐ πάνυ τὰ λαμπρὰ δύναται βλέπειν recalls the experience of the newly
escaped prisoner from the cave in Plato's *Resp.* 516a, where we have a similar hierarchy of objects to observe before it is possible to view the sun
itself. This culminating vision is, in fact, for Plotinus a complete identification of the self with the light of the sun, as expressed in line 18: ὅλος αὐτὸς
φῶς ἀληθινὸν μόνον.

9,5. ἴδε. Note how once again the use of the intimate second-person singular is resumed.

9,7. ἄναγε ἐπὶ σαυτὸν καὶ ἴδε. With this important injunction Plotinus tells
us that intellectual and spiritual awareness are produced not merely by
external stimuli but, more importantly, by looking into our inner selves
and making the soul like its objects, in this case by making the soul beautiful so that it can more fully perceive beauty. This idea has already occurred
in 1.3,3–4, where soul is said to "make a statement by fitting [what it sees]
with the form in it." We can compare this with Plotinus's ethical theory,
which implies that ethical conduct is both a prerequisite *and* a consequence
of contemplative progress. See Smith 1974, 76–77. See also 5.8,2,41–46 for
the same idea of seeing oneself beautiful within.

9,8–15. The long flow of this sentence expresses well the long, continuous,
and relentless effort required to bring the inner self into harmony with the
divine. It is not without rhetorical flourishes:

ὅσα σκολιά, ὅσα σκοτεινὰ καθαίρων ἐργάζου εἶναι λαμπρὰ
καὶ μὴ παύσῃ τεκταίνων τὸ σὸν ἄγαλμα, ἕως ἂν ἐκλάμ-
ψειέ σοι τῆς ἀρετῆς ἡ θεοειδὴς ἀγλαΐα, ἕως ἂν ἴδῃς σωφροσύνην ἐν ἁγνῷ βεβῶσαν βάθρῳ. Εἰ γέγονας τοῦτο   15

---

tricolon with lengthened third member:
     ἀφαιρεῖ … ἀπέξεσε … ἐποίησεν
     ἀφαίρει … ἀπεύθυνε … ἐργάζου
chiasmus: ἀπεύθυνε ὅσα σκολιά, ὅσα σκοτεινὰ … ἐργάζου
repetition: ἕως ἔδειξε … ἕως ἂν ἐκλάμψειε … ἕως ἂν ἴδῃς

9,13. τεκταίνων τὸ σὸν ἄγαλμα. Cf. Plato, *Phaedr.* 252d7: καὶ ὡς θεὸν αὐτὸν
ἐκεῖνον ὄντα ἑαυτῷ οἷον ἄγαλμα τεκταίνεται. In Plato, however, the statue is
not the inner self but an image of the beloved, the object of physical desire.
See Armstrong 1961, 112. A similar idea is found in 4.7[2]10,44–47:
"For the soul does not, of course, 'see wisdom and justice' [Plato, *Phaedr.*
247d6] by making excursions but by contemplation within itself of itself
and of what it was formerly, seeing them firmly fixed within itself like statues that have become tarnished with the passage of time and which it has
now burnished" (Fleet). A comparable idea is found in Porphyry, *Marc.*
11.112,2–5: "The wise man … must prepare by his wisdom a sanctuary for
god in his mind, adorning it with a living statue, intellect, in which god
has impressed his image" (Des Places); and in the fifth-century Platonist
Hierocles of Alexandria, *Commentary on the Golden Verses of Pythagoras*:
"He alone knows how to honor [the gods] who does not contaminate the
dignity of those who are honored, and who makes it his foremost concern
to present himself as a sanctuary, and works to make his own soul a divine
statue and prepares his own intellect as a temple to receive the divine light"
(31,21–32,4 Mullach).

9,14–15. σωφροσύνην ἐν ἁγνῷ βεβῶσαν βάθρῳ. Cf. Plato, *Phaedr.* 254b6–7:
μετὰ σωφροσύνης ἐν ἁγνῷ βεβῶσαν βάθρῳ.

9,15. εἰ γέγονας τοῦτο. See also lines 21 and 23. The notion of becoming
identical with the object of striving or contemplation is central to Plotinus. It is another expression of the idea that true knowledge is attained
only when the thinking subject is identical with the object of its thinking
(for which see 5.5.1–2). This is valid not only for the hypostasis Intellect

καὶ εἶδες αὐτὸ καὶ σαυτῷ καθαρὸς συνεγένου οὐδὲν ἔχων
ἐμπόδιον πρὸς τὸ εἰς οὕτω γενέσθαι οὐδὲ σὺν αὐτῷ ἄλλο τι
ἐντὸς μεμιγμένον ἔχων, ἀλλ' ὅλος αὐτὸς φῶς ἀληθινὸν μόνον,
οὐ μεγέθει μεμετρημένον οὐδὲ σχήματι εἰς ἐλάττωσιν πε-
ριγραφὲν οὐδ' αὖ εἰς μέγεθος δι' ἀπειρίας αὐξηθέν, ἀλλ'   20
ἀμέτρητον πανταχοῦ, ὡς ἂν μεῖζον παντὸς μέτρου καὶ παντὸς
κρεῖσσον ποσοῦ· εἰ τοῦτο γενόμενον σαυτὸν ἴδοις, ὄψις ἤδη
γενόμενος θαρσήσας περὶ σαυτῷ καὶ ἐνταῦθα ἤδη ἀναβε-
βηκὼς μηκέτι τοῦ δεικνύντος δεηθεὶς ἀτενίσας ἴδε· οὗτος   25
γὰρ μόνος ὁ ὀφθαλμὸς τὸ μέγα κάλλος βλέπει. Ἐὰν δὲ ἴη
ἐπὶ τὴν θέαν λημῶν κακίαις καὶ οὐ κεκαθαρμένος ἢ
ἀσθενής, ἀνανδρίᾳ οὐ δυνάμενος τὰ πάνυ λαμπρὰ βλέπειν,
οὐδὲν βλέπει, κἂν ἄλλος δεικνύῃ παρὸν τὸ ὁραθῆναι δυνά-

---

but also for the intellect of the individual. This becomes even more complex when viewed dynamically, when Plotinus considers the ascent of the individual within the different levels of his or her own being, from that of perception to discursive reason (vested in the rational soul) and from discursive reason to intellection. For this transition to complete identity of subject and object at the level of our intellect, one may consult the first part of 5.3, already cited at 6,13 where it was noted that Plotinus uses the verb γίγνεσθαι three times to indicate that, in becoming intellect, we "become" completely other than what we were before.

9,22–24. The accumulation of participles in this sentence is a particularity of Plotinus's condensed style of writing.

9,24. τοῦ δεικνύντος. Having no further use of a guide marks the point of transition from discursive reasoning, whether done privately or in the teaching context of the philosophical school, to a direct encounter with the object sought. See also 6.9.4,14–15 where, in speaking of the One, he says that before we have a personal encounter with it our discursive reason can only point the way (ὥσπερ ὁδὸν δεικνύντες) rather than give explicit directions, for teaching goes only so far as the road and the traveling (μέχρι γὰρ τῆς ὁδοῦ καὶ τῆς πορείας ἡ δίδαξις), after which personal vision must be engaged (ἡ δὲ θέα αὐτοῦ ἔργον ἤδη τοῦ ἰδεῖν βεβουλημένου).

μενον. Τὸ γὰρ ὁρῶν πρὸς τὸ ὁρώμενον συγγενὲς καὶ ὅμοιον
ποιησάμενον δεῖ ἐπιβάλλειν τῇ θέᾳ. Οὐ γὰρ ἂν πώποτε   30
εἶδεν ὀφθαλμὸς ἥλιον ἡλιοειδὴς μὴ γεγενημένος, οὐδὲ τὸ
καλὸν ἂν ἴδοι ψυχὴ μὴ καλὴ γενομένη. Γενέσθω δὴ πρῶτον θεοειδὴς πᾶς καὶ καλὸς πᾶς, εἰ μέλλει θεάσασθαι θεόν
τε καὶ καλόν. Ἥξει γὰρ πρῶτον ἀναβαίνων ἐπὶ τὸν νοῦν
κἀκεῖ πάντα εἴσεται καλὰ τὰ εἴδη καὶ φήσει τὸ κάλλος   35
τοῦτο εἶναι, τὰς ἰδέας· πάντα γὰρ ταύταις καλά, τοῖς
νοῦ γεννήμασι καὶ οὐσίας. Τὸ δὲ ἐπέκεινα τούτου τὴν
τοῦ ἀγαθοῦ λέγομεν φύσιν προβεβλημένον τὸ καλὸν πρὸ
αὑτῆς ἔχουσαν. Ὥστε ὁλοσχερεῖ μὲν λόγῳ τὸ πρῶτον

9,29. The most natural grammatical "subject" of this sentence (i.e., with
the impersonal δεῖ) would be τὸ ὁρῶν, but τὸν ὀφθαλμὸν or even τινα is
possible.

9,35. πάντα … καλά: πάντα and καλά are to be taken as predicative of
τὰ εἴδη: "all of them beautiful." The identity of beauty with the Ideas, the
contents of Nous as a whole, as affirmed in 6,21, is once again expressed
by the transition from all the Forms individually (πάντα τὰ εἴδη) to their
identification as a single whole, τοῦτο: "and he will say that this is Beauty,
the Ideas."

9,36–37. τοῖς … οὐσίας is in apposition to ταύταις. By describing the Ideas
as the product of Intellect, Plotinus is probably thinking both of the gen-
eration of the Ideas within Intellect as its essential activity of thinking and
of the external effect of Intellect, through the Ideas, on all that is below it,
which makes them beautiful (πάντα γὰρ ταύταις καλά), beginning with
soul and the physical universe. For the soul as the product of Intellect, see
V.1.7,42: νοῦ δὲ γέννημα λόγος τις.

9,39–43. ὥστε ὁλοσχερεῖ μὲν λογῷ τὸ πρῶτον καλόν…: "so in a rough
sense it [the One] is the primal beauty.…" Can the One (the Good) be
also termed "the Beautiful'? The same question arises in the treatise *On
the Categories* (6.2[43].18) and *On the Forms and the Good* (6.7[38].22),
both composed in a later period. Clearly the question, which appears to be
dismissed rather cursorily here in 1.6, is of some importance to Plotinus.
In fact, it raises difficult issues about ascribing positive characteristics to

καλόν· διαιρῶν δὲ τὰ νοητὰ τὸ μὲν νοητὸν καλὸν τὸν τῶν   40
εἰδῶν φήσει τόπον, τὸ δ' ἀγαθὸν τὸ ἐπέκεινα καὶ πηγὴν
καὶ ἀρχὴν τοῦ καλοῦ. Ἡ ἐν τῷ αὐτῷ τἀγαθὸν καὶ

---

the nature of the One as ultimate principle. In 6.2 Plotinus seems happy
enough to identify Beauty with Being, although he does initially suggest
(18,1–4) that one might locate it somewhat higher, either with the One
itself or rather with something "shining out from it" (οἷον ἀπόστιλβον):
"As for the beautiful [τοῦ καλοῦ], if the primary Beauty [ἡ καλλονὴ] is that
[transcendent First], what could be said about it would be the same and
similar to what was said about the Good; and if it is that which, one might
say, shines out upon the Idea [of beauty], [one would say that it is not the
same in all] the Forms and that the shining on them is posterior." In 6.7
Plotinus goes into greater detail; in chapter 22, while placing beauty at the
level of Intellect, he suggests that it receives from the One a kind of illu-
mination that gives life to that beauty (ἀργόν τε γὰρ τὸ κάλλος αὐτου, πρὶν
τοῦ ἀγαθοῦ φῶς λάβῃ 6.7.22,11–12). It should be noted that, as in 1.6, the
immediate context for these remarks is the ascent of the individual soul
and its experience of something above Intellect. But not content with this
explanation, Plotinus returns once again to the same issue in chapter 32,
where he refers to the Good (the One) as παντὸς καλοῦ ἄνθος (32,31) and
states that its beauty is of a different order that is beyond beauty (32,28–29:
τὸ κάλλος αὐτοῦ ἄλλον τρόπον καὶ κάλλος ὑπὲρ κάλλος) and in that "the primary beautiful, then, and the First is without form, and Beauty [ἡ καλλονὴ]
is that, the nature of the Good" (33,21–23). Nothing could more clearly
express Plotinus's difficulty in delineating the nature of the One, which he
wants to be not merely the cause of all that is beneath it but also in some
way to be the totality of everything that exists, an idea most graphically
expressed in the opening sentence of 5.2[11]: "The One is all things and
not a single one of them; it is the principle of all things, not all things, but
all things in a transcendent way; for in a sense they do occur in the One"
(1,1–2). For a more detailed discussion of these passages concerning the
location of Beauty, see Smith 2014.

9,40. διαιρῶν. Supply an indefinite subject: "if one makes distinctions in
the intelligible world."

καλὸν πρῶτον θήσεται· πλὴν ἐκεῖ τὸ καλόν.

9,43. πλὴν: an adverb meaning "in any case." In other words, even if we do put Beauty and the Good on the same level (the One), beauty is still to be found in the intelligible world (ἐκεῖ).

5.8. *On Intelligible Beauty*

Chapter 1

How can we contemplate the beauty of Intellect? Although the way we do this (initially through the contemplation of physical beauty) may recall the earlier treatise 1.6, *On Beauty*, Plotinus is more concerned in the present treatise with the nature of Intellect itself (and its consequences for the status and value of the physical universe) than with Intellect as the goal of our own spiritual journey. Nevertheless, these first two chapters serve to enrich and expand our understanding of Plotinus's appreciation of physical beauty. To establish the nature of the beauty of the intelligible world, he begins by tracing the cause of beauty in the physical world, commencing with the beauty of manufactured objects. The Platonic notion of art as imitation is expressed positively in terms of his own interpretation of Platonic metaphysics, in which all production is seen as a product of contemplation (3.8), each product being a successively lower image of its maker or cause, but all, even the lowest, depending on the first cause.

5.8. ΠΕΡΙ ΤΟΥ ΝΟΗΤΟΥ ΚΑΛΛΟΥΣ

1. Ἐπειδή φαμεν τὸν ἐν θέᾳ τοῦ νοητοῦ κόσμου γεγενη-
μένον καὶ τὸ τοῦ ἀληθινοῦ νοῦ κατανοήσαντα κάλλος τοῦτον δυνήσεσθαι καὶ τὸν τούτου πατέρα καὶ τὸν ἐπέκεινα
νοῦ εἰς ἔννοιαν βαλέσθαι, πειραθῶμεν ἰδεῖν καὶ εἰπεῖν ἡμῖν
αὐτοῖς, ὡς οἷόν τε τὰ τοιαῦτα εἰπεῖν, πῶς ἄν τις τὸ   5

1,1–4. The opening sentence refers to the concluding two chapters of 3.8, in which Plotinus explains how contemplation leads to Intellect and the source and cause of Intellect, "that which is simply one" (3.8.10, 22), which is identified with the Good (3.8.12). The treatise 5.8, in fact, forms the second part of a large tractate that was divided and given separate titles by Porphyry. It comprised, apart from the present tractate, *On Contemplation* (3.8[30]), *That the Intelligibles Are Not External to the Intellect and the Good* (5.5[32]) and *Against the Gnostics* (2.9[33]), its grand aim being to provide a convincing account of the intelligible origin of a physical world that is worthy, in its beauty and goodness, of its transcendent source.

1,2. τοῦ ἀληθινοῦ νοῦ. The description of intellect here as ἀληθινός serves to emphasize that Plotinus is dealing with intellect at its highest level, at which intellect and object of thought are one, for Plotinus sometimes uses the term νοῦς more loosely of the activity of soul at the higher levels of discursive thought (e.g., 6.2.7,40).

1,3. τούτου πατέρα. The father of Intellect is the One, which "transcends" it. The phraseology recalls the Good that is ἐπέκεινα τῆς οὐσίας in Plato, *Resp.* 509b9.

1,4. βαλέσθαι is middle. Cf. the Homeric usage, for example, ἐνὶ θυμῷ βάλλεαι in *Il.* 20.195–196.

1,4–5. ἡμῖν αὐτοῖς. It is clear from these words that the work as a whole is addressed to members of Plotinus's own school rather than as a general polemic aimed at gnostics at large; perhaps, then a warning to those students of his who might have had gnostic leanings, which included a tendency to disparage the goodness and beauty to be found in the physical universe.

κάλλος τοῦ νοῦ καὶ τοῦ κόσμου ἐκείνου θεάσαιτο. Κειμένων τοίνυν ἀλλήλων ἐγγύς, ἔστω δέ, εἰ βούλει, <δύο> λίθων
ἐν ὄγκῳ, τοῦ μὲν ἀρρυθμίστου καὶ τέχνης ἀμοίρου, τοῦ δὲ
ἤδη τέχνῃ κεκρατημένου εἰς ἄγαλμα θεοῦ ἢ καί τινος
ἀνθρώπου, θεοῦ μὲν Χάριτος ἤ τινος Μούσης, ἀνθρώπου   10
δὲ μή τινος, ἀλλ' ὃν ἐκ πάντων καλῶν πεποίηκεν ἡ τέχνη,
φανείη μὲν ἂν ὁ ὑπὸ τῆς τέχνης γεγενημένος εἰς εἴδους
κάλλος καλὸς οὐ παρὰ τὸ εἶναι λίθος—ἦν γὰρ ἂν καὶ ὁ
ἕτερος ὁμοίως καλός—ἀλλὰ παρὰ τοῦ εἴδους, ὃ ἐνῆκεν ἡ
τέχνη. Τοῦτο μὲν τοίνυν τὸ εἶδος οὐκ εἶχεν ἡ ὕλη, ἀλλ' ἦν   15

1,5. οἷόν τε. Supply the verb εἰμί (ὄν or ἐστί).

1,7. ἐγγύς governs ἀλλήλων, the whole phrase adverbally qualifying κειμένων ... δύο λίθων, genitives that in turn are dependent on ὁ ὑπὸ τῆς τέχνης γεγενημένος [λίθος] (1,12) and ὁ ἕτερος [λίθος] (1,13–14): "of two stones lying near each other ... the one...."

1,10. Statues of the Graces and the Muses were quite commonplace. Plotinus may also have been aware of the sort of allegorization of the Graces to which the Stoic philosopher Chrysippus dedicated a whole book, according to Seneca (*Ben.* 1.3). Diogenes Laertius also tells us (*Vit. phil.* 4.1) that Plato dedicated a shrine to the Muses in the Academy grove, to which Speusippus later added statues of the Graces.

1,11. ἐκ πάντων καλῶν. Plotinus has in mind not a particular person (τινος ἀνθρώπου) but an idealized portrayal of which every part and component is beautiful. See, at the conclusion of this chapter, the example of Pheidias, whose inspiration comes from contemplating the transcendent form of Zeus rather than physical models.

1,12. φανείη μέν is contrasted with ἦν δ ' ἐν τῷ δημιουργῷ (1,16–17): the "appearance" of beauty in the worked stone as opposed to the form of beauty in the artist.

1,14. ἐνῆκεν: aorist (active) of ἐνίημι.

ἐν τῷ ἐννοήσαντι καὶ πρὶν ἐλθεῖν εἰς τὸν λίθον· ἦν δ’ ἐν τῷ
δημιουργῷ οὐ καθόσον ὀφθαλμοὶ ἢ χεῖρες ἦσαν αὐτῷ, ἀλλ’
ὅτι μετεῖχε τῆς τέχνης. Ἦν ἄρα ἐν τῇ τέχνῃ τὸ κάλλος
τοῦτο ἄμεινον πολλῷ· οὐ γὰρ ἐκεῖνο ἦλθεν εἰς τὸν λίθον τὸ
ἐν τῇ τέχνῃ, ἀλλ’ ἐκεῖνο μὲν μένει, ἄλλο δὲ ἀπ’ ἐκείνης   20
ἔλαττον ἐκείνου· καὶ οὐδὲ τοῦτο ἔμεινε καθαρὸν ἐν αὐτῷ,
οὐδὲ οἷον ἐβούλετο, ἀλλ’ ὅσον εἶξεν ὁ λίθος τῇ τέχνῃ. Εἰ

1,16. ἐν τῷ ἐννοήσαντι. Not in the sense that it is a fabrication of the artist.
The artist's concept is itself an objectively existing form, as we see from
the following words: ἦν ἄρα ἐν τῇ τέχνῃ τὸ κάλλος (1,18). In this respect,
the beauty of artistic creations, in the end, depends, as does the beauty
of natural things, on the same level of objective causes: the transcendent
forms of the intelligible world.

1,18. μετεῖχε. μετέχειν is the Platonic expression for the participation of
sensibles in forms. Here it is applied to the participation of the artist in the
form of beauty, which lies above him.

1,20. ἄλλο δὲ. Supply ἦλθεν εἰς τὸν λίθον.

Similar ideas are found also in 5.9[5].5,36–42, where Plotinus refers to
this "remaining" of the transcendent form (and to natural and artistic
creation): "The objects of sense are what they are called by participation,
since their underlying nature receives its shape from elsewhere: bronze,
for instance, from the art of sculpture and wood from the art of carpentry,
the art passing into them through an image but itself remaining in self-
identity outside matter [διὰ εἰδώλου τῆς τέχνης εἰς αὐτὰ ἰούσης, τῆς δὲ τέχνης
αὐτῆς ἔξω ὕλης ἐν ταὐτότητι μενούσης] and possessing the true statue or bed
[cf. Plato, Resp. 597c3]. This is also true of [natural] bodies."

1,21. ἐν αὐτῷ. That is, ἐν τῷ λίθῳ.

1,22. ἐβούλετο. Supply ὁ δημιουργός as subject.

ὅσον εἶξεν ὁ λίθος τῇ τέχνῃ. The suitability (ἐπιτηδειότης) of a substrate to
receive form or powers is a constant theme in Plotinus and runs parallel with the idea that powers diminish as they descend from the highest

δ' ἡ τέχνη ὅ ἐστι καὶ ἔχει τοιοῦτο ποιεῖ—καλὸν δὲ ποιεῖ
κατὰ λόγον οὗ ποιεῖ—μειζόνως καὶ ἀληθεστέρως καλή ἐστι
τὸ κάλλος ἔχουσα τὸ τέχνης μεῖζον μέντοι καὶ κάλλιον, ἢ   25
ὅσον ἐστὶν ἐν τῷ ἔξω. Καὶ γὰρ ὅσῳ ἰὸν εἰς τὴν ὕλην ἐκτέ-

---

to the lowest levels. The two may be seen in this paragraph, where just
a little later Plotinus speaks of the diminishing power of levels of beauty
as an example of a more general principle. These two principles provide
Plotinus with an explanation for the imperfections of this world compared
with its transcendent model. But an immediate problem with matter as a
restrictive component is that it seems to provide it with a positive force of
obstruction, whereas Plotinus is elsewhere (see 2.4.13–14) concerned to
remove all qualities from matter.

1,23. The sentence should be understood as follows: ἡ τέχνη ποιεῖ [τὸν
λίθον] τοιοῦτο ὅ ἐστι καὶ ἔχει [ἡ τέχνη]: "makes it such as it is and possesses
itself." By making τέχνη, rather than the artist, the subject, Plotinus wants
to stress that the idea in the artist's mind is more important than the physical effort of creation. Thus, in the previous lines, he has said that the artist
is properly said to make because he shares in art and not by his eyes and
hands.

ἐστι καὶ ἔχει. Art both *is* beautiful and *possesses* beauty, the latter because
there is a form of beauty yet higher even than the one that art possesses.

1,24. οὗ ποιεῖ. τούτου ὅ, "in conformity with the rational principle of that
which it is making," that is, the form that it possesses and that it seeks to
impose on matter. But the finished product is less perfect than the form
with which art operates.

1,25. ἔχουσα is causal: "since it possess the beauty of art that is greater...."

1,26–32. Degrees of unity are paralleled by degrees of power and reality
in a world that becomes increasingly more pluralized as it unfolds, until it
projects itself three-dimensionally in matter.

τάται, τόσῳ ἀσθενέστερον τοῦ ἐν ἑνὶ μένοντος. Ἀφίσταται
γὰρ ἑαυτοῦ πᾶν διιστάμενον, εἰ ἰσχύς, ἐν ἰσχύι, εἰ θερμό-
της, ἐν θερμότητι, εἰ ὅλως δύναμις, ἐν δυνάμει, εἰ κάλλος,
ἐν κάλλει. Καὶ τὸ πρῶτον ποιοῦν πᾶν καθ᾽ αὑτὸ κρεῖττον   30
εἶναι δεῖ τοῦ ποιουμένου· οὐ γὰρ ἡ ἀμουσία μουσικόν, ἀλλ᾽
ἡ μουσική, καὶ τὴν ἐν αἰσθητῷ ἡ πρὸ τούτου. Εἰ δέ τις τὰς
τέχνας ἀτιμάζει, ὅτι μιμούμεναι τὴν φύσιν ποιοῦσι, πρῶτον

1,27–28. ἀφίσταται … ἑαυτοῦ is a common expression in Plotinus; "to
draw apart from oneself" is "to cease to be what one is."

1,30. πᾶν: "in every case," that is, every first mover. Plotinus is thinking
here of primary causes in general, as the following sentence illustrates,
rather than a single ultimate primary cause such as the One.

1,31–32. ἀμουσία. This seems an odd example to illustrate the principle
enunciated in the previous lines, that powers diminish. Perhaps Plotinus
wants to stress that the inferiority of music in the sensible world compared to that of the intelligible world (including the music of the spheres)
is not primarily caused by the imperfections of sensible media but rather
the diminishing power of music as it descends to lower levels from its
transcendent cause. This would suggest, then, a correction to the initial
reference (1,22) to the apparent recalcitrance of the physical medium (of
stone).

1,32–40. εἰ δέ τις τὰς τέχνας ἀτιμάζει…. We may immediately think of
Plato's criticism in *Resp.* 597bff. of imitation in art. But would Plotinus have
criticized Plato so directly? Plotinus regarded himself as a Platonist and
placed Plato as the focal point and supreme exponent of what he regarded
as a single definitive philosophical system, one that still needed clarifica-
tion (see 5.1.8,10–14), but that should not contradict it (6.4.16,4–7). He
does, however, sometimes seem to leave room for debate (2.9.6,43–52).
Rist (1967, 183–87) thinks his view on imitation is a direct criticism of
Plato, Armstrong (1974, 179) that he was probably not fully aware that
he was contradicting Plato. On balance, it seems more likely that he here
has in mind those who, in his view, have misinterpreted the Platonic text.
The notion that the artist has direct access to the intelligible model can be
traced back at least to the first century BCE: Cicero, *Or. Brut.* 8–10; Seneca,

μὲν φατέον καὶ τὰς φύσεις μιμεῖσθαι ἄλλα. Ἔπειτα δεῖ
εἰδέναι, ὡς οὐχ ἁπλῶς τὸ ὁρώμενον μιμοῦνται, ἀλλ᾽ ἀνα-   35
τρέχουσιν ἐπὶ τοὺς λόγους, ἐξ ὧν ἡ φύσις. Εἶτα καὶ ὅτι
πολλὰ παρ᾽ αὐτῶν ποιοῦσι καὶ προστιθέασι δέ, ὅτῳ τι
ἐλλείπει, ὡς ἔχουσαι τὸ κάλλος. Ἐπεὶ καὶ ὁ Φειδίας τὸν
Δία πρὸς οὐδὲν αἰσθητὸν ποιήσας, ἀλλὰ λαβὼν οἷος ἂν
γένοιτο, εἰ ἡμῖν ὁ Ζεὺς δι᾽ ὀμμάτων ἐθέλοι φανῆναι.   40

Ep. 65.7–10; Alcinous, *Didask.* 163,21–23; Philostratus, *Vit. Apoll.* 6.19.2;
see the discussion in Theiler 1934, 15ff. See further the introduction above,
p. 10.

1,34. καὶ τὰς φύσεις μιμεῖσθαι ἄλλα. That is, the whole of the physical universe is an imitation of its intelligible model.

1,37. παρ᾽ αὐτῶν. The artist not only goes back to the perfect intelligible
form of man but adds something. This is a remarkable tribute to the creative genius of the artist. A similar idea in the general production of nature
may be seen in 6.7.9,40–46, where Plotinus describes the unfolding of the
form of horse from its intelligible model to its natural physical manifestation. At this final stage, additional elements (e.g., nails and horns) develop
to compensate for the deficiencies experienced in the progressive diminu-
tion in power of the unfolding form.

καὶ ... δέ: "and ... moreover," "and even...."

Chapter 2

The inquiry now moves to the cause of beauty in natural physical phenomena. The origin of their beauty, as in the case of the beauty of works of art, will also be found in transcendent form. Plotinus argues that, if the experience of beauty does not come from the externality or mass of an object, it must come from something immaterial. We then add to this that nature or "logos," the producing agent, must itself be beautiful. He then returns to the ultimate purpose of this discussion of physical beauty: our own personal discovery of the transcendent beauty within our own souls.

2. Ἀλλ' ἡμῖν ἀφείσθωσαν αἱ τέχναι· ὧν δὲ λέγονται τὰ
ἔργα μιμεῖσθαι, τὰ φύσει κάλλη γινόμενα καὶ λεγόμενα,
θεωρῶμεν, λογικά τε ζῷα καὶ ἄλογα πάντα καὶ μάλιστα
ὅσα κατώρθωται αὐτῶν τοῦ πλάσαντος αὐτὰ καὶ δημιουργήσαντος ἐπικρατήσαντος τῆς ὕλης καὶ εἶδος ὃ ἐβούλετο   5
παρασχόντος. Τί οὖν τὸ κάλλος ἐστὶν ἐν τούτοις; Οὐ γὰρ
δὴ τὸ αἷμα καὶ τὰ καταμήνια· ἀλλὰ καὶ χρόα ἄλλη τού-

2,1. ἀφείσθωσαν: third-person plural, perfect passive imperative, with dative of the agent. For the form, see Plato, *Leg.* 764a7: ἀζήμιος ἀφείσθω.

2,2–3. The list of beautiful physical objects needs some explaining. It is rather surprising that Plotinus introduces gods and goddesses and even more so those that are not visible. But their relevance becomes apparent with the introduction of the *Phaedrus* myth in chapter 4. Why is it limited to ζῷα (living beings, whether "rational," i.e., human, or "irrational," i.e., animals), since it is implied in 1,13–14 that a stone can be beautiful as stone? From a later treatise (6.7[38]) we may infer that Plotinus could have expanded the range to include things and processes that we would regard as totally inanimate, for in arguing that the intelligible world has the patterns of everything within it including plants, he concludes, "the growth, then, and the shaping of stones and the inner patterning of mountains as they grow one must most certainly suppose take place because an ensouled forming principle is working within them and giving them form; and this is the active form of the earth, like what is called the growth-nature in trees" (6.7.11,24–28). If we take into account the close connection of 5.8 with 3.8, where Plotinus implies that even the most basic levels of existence possess some rudimentary kind of life and cognitive activity, it is plausible that ζῷα in this passage could have a more inclusive meaning.

2,4–6. τοῦ πλάσαντος … παρασχόντος. ἐπικρατήσαντος and παρασχόντος form a genitive absolute with τοῦ πλάσαντος and δημιουργήσαντος as subjects.

2,7. In rejecting purely material principles as responsible for structuring bodies, Plotinus may here have Aristotle in mind, who in *Part. an.* 651a14–15 makes blood the ultimate nourishment and matter for bodies and in *Gen. an.* 729a32 equates the menstrual fluids with "primary matter."

των καὶ σχῆμα ἢ οὐδὲν ἤ τι ἄσχημον ἢ οἷον τὸ περιέχον
ἁπλοῦν τι, οἷα ὕλη. Πόθεν δὴ ἐξέλαμψε τὸ τῆς Ἑλένης
τῆς περιμαχήτου κάλλος, ἢ ὅσαι γυναικῶν Ἀφροδίτης   10
ὅμοιαι κάλλει; Ἐπεὶ καὶ τὸ τῆς Ἀφροδίτης αὐτῆς πόθεν,
ἢ εἴ τις ὅλως καλὸς ἄνθρωπος ἢ θεὸς τῶν ἂν εἰς ὄψιν

2,7–9. ἀλλὰ καὶ.… Plotinus then goes on to reject as insufficient conventional explanations of beauty, such as color and shape, as in 1.6.1,20–21. The Greek here is not easy and seems to be corrupt. I translate as follows: "But the beauty of natural things is also not their color, which is always changing [ἄλλη], nor their external shape. It is either nothing or something without shape or something simple like that which circumscribes," taking it in the same way as Laurent (2002): "ce n'est pas non plus leur couleur, qui est différente dans chaque cas, ni leur figure extérieure. Ou bien.…" Armstrong translates: "rather, the colour of these [blood and menstrual fluid] is different and their shape is either no shape or a shapeless shape or like that which delimits something simple." To construe σχῆμα with ἄσχημον (their shape is no shape) does not seem to yield a helpful concept. I suggest punctuating after σχῆμα and extending the concept of change involved in ἄλλη to σχῆμα (σχῆμα ἄλλον: the shape of natural objects is, like color, also variable). The following sentence then reduces the choices to three alternatives: nothing, something without shape, or "something simple like that which circumscribes" (τὸ περιέχον). The first is clearly inadmissible, the absence of shape suggests the incorporeal in general (see Plato, *Phaedr.* 247c6–7, where true being has neither color nor shape: ἀσχημάτιστος), whereas "something simple like that which circumscribes" suggests an incorporeal power such as soul (see 4.3.20,15 where soul contains [περιέχον] rather than is contained), indicating here something that has the power to impose limit or shape of some kind but is itself simple, that is, incorporeal, since it is without shape, which is a characteristic of body. This all leads up to the identification of the cause of beauty as an active power, that is, form, in line 14.

2,10. Ἀφροδίτης. ὅμοιος may be followed by either a genitive or a dative.

2,12–14. The visible gods referred to here are probably the stars (see 3.2.14,25–30 and 2.9.5,4–14), and the gods who are not visible but whose beauty can be seen may refer to the gods of traditional mythology whose

ἐλθόντων ἢ καὶ μὴ ἰόντων, ἐχόντων δὲ ἐπ᾽ αὐτοῖς ὁραθὲν
ἂν κάλλος; Ἆρ᾽ οὐκ εἶδος μὲν πανταχοῦ τοῦτο, ἧκον δὲ
ἐπὶ τὸ γενόμενον ἐκ τοῦ ποιήσαντος, ὥσπερ ἐν ταῖς τέχναις   15
ἐλέγετο ἐπὶ τὰ τεχνητὰ ἰέναι παρὰ τῶν τεχνῶν; Τί οὖν;
Καλὰ μὲν τὰ ποιήματα καὶ ὁ ἐπὶ τῆς ὕλης λόγος, ὁ δὲ μὴ
ἐν ὕλῃ, ἀλλ᾽ ἐν τῷ ποιοῦντι λόγος οὐ κάλλος, ὁ πρῶτος καὶ
ἄυλος [ἀλλ᾽ εἰς ἕν] οὗτος; Ἀλλ᾽ εἰ μὲν ὁ ὄγκος ἦν καλός,
καθόσον ὄγκος ἦν, ἐχρῆν τὸν λόγον, ὅτι μὴ ἦν ὄγκος, τὸν   20
ποιήσαντα μὴ καλὸν εἶναι· εἰ δέ, ἐάν τε ἐν σμικρῷ ἐάν τε
ἐν μεγάλῳ τὸ αὐτὸ εἶδος ᾖ, ὁμοίως κινεῖ καὶ διατίθησι τὴν

form is sometimes revealed to humans in theophanies or in works of art
(such as Phidias's statue of Zeus) and in literature.

2,12–14. ἂν εἰς ὄψιν ἐλθόντων ... ὁραθὲν ἂν. ἂν is retained when an "original"
potential (ἂν = optative) or general clause (ἂν + subjunctive) is expressed
by a participle.

2,18. κάλλος rather than καλόν, to emphasize the difference in status
between the transcendent cause of beauty and the beauty immanent in
bodies.

2,20. καθόσον ὄγκος ἦν. That is, when taken without any consideration
of even the most basic form imposed on it. The bare stone, for example,
in chapter 1, already displays form in its shape, color, and texture. Mass
(ὄγκος) is what is "prior" to this. It differs, too, from matter in that it represents for Plotinus the three-dimensionality that is the contribution of pure
matter to the constitution of physical objects, that is, the mode in which the
immanent forms express themselves in matter. If mass (or indeed matter)
were said to be beautiful, we would be designating as beautiful something
that was in itself devoid of form and thereby excluding rational principle
that is the provider of form as a cause of beauty. It is clear from the following lines that Plotinus does not regard the magnitude of objects and their
physicality, for example, their resistance, as the product of form but rather
as characteristics of mass. What gives shape and beauty to objects is their
immanent form, and it is this form that we perceive rather than the mass
of the object. Even size is not perceived by us as the mass-size of an object,
but its size is perceived as a form (2,27–28).

ψυχὴν τὴν τοῦ ὁρῶντος τῇ αὐτοῦ δυνάμει, τὸ κάλλος οὐ
τῷ τοῦ ὄγκου μεγέθει ἀποδοτέον. Τεκμήριον δὲ καὶ τόδε,
ὅτι ἔξω μὲν ἕως ἐστίν, οὔπω εἴδομεν, ὅταν δὲ εἴσω γένηται,   25
διέθηκεν. Εἴσεισι δὲ δι’ ὀμμάτων εἶδος ὂν μόνον· ἢ πῶς διὰ
σμικροῦ; Συνεφέλκεται δὲ καὶ τὸ μέγεθος οὐ μέγα ἐν ὄγκῳ,
ἀλλ’ εἴδει γενόμενον μέγα. Ἔπειτα ἢ αἰσχρὸν δεῖ τὸ ποιοῦν
ἢ ἀδιάφορον ἢ καλὸν εἶναι. Αἰσχρὸν μὲν οὖν ὂν οὐκ ἂν
τὸ ἐναντίον ποιήσειεν, ἀδιάφορον δὲ τί μᾶλλον καλὸν ἢ   30
αἰσχρόν; Ἀλλὰ γάρ ἐστι καὶ ἡ φύσις ἡ τὰ οὕτω καλὰ
δημιουργοῦσα πολὺ πρότερον καλή, ἡμεῖς δὲ τῶν ἔνδον
οὐδὲν ὁρᾶν εἰθισμένοι οὐδ’ εἰδότες τὸ ἔξω διώκομεν ἀγνο-

2,25. ἔξω μὲν ἕως ἐστίν. An object that has not yet impinged upon and transmitted itself though our sense organs to the faculty of perception.

2,26. διέθηκεν used absolutely. Supply ἡμᾶς.
μόνον. That is, form alone without any material component.

2,27–28, συνεφέλκεται δὲ καὶ τὸ μέγεθος … εἴδει γενόμενον μέγα. This indicates that the object as perceived, although entirely constituted of forms, is perceived *as an object with physical properties* and is thus different from the ideal, which is without such manifested physical properties.

2,28. τὸ ποιοῦν. The argument now moves from form to the maker. ποιοῦν, εἶδος, and λόγος are different aspects of the creative power that ultimately originates from the One and is manifested most fully at the level of Intellect. Sometimes Plotinus wants to distinguish these different aspects while still maintaining their essential unity, so in this passage the discussion moves from rational principle and form to the maker in line 29.

2,30–31. τί μᾶλλον καλὸν ἢ αἰσχρόν: Supply ἂν ποιήσειεν.

2,31. φύσις: Sometimes φύσις (e.g., in 3.8) is given almost the status of a hypostasis, on a level just beneath that of the world soul, but here it refers to the rational principle that produces the physical world, and the term φύσις simply reminds us that the subject of the chapter is the natural world as opposed to the products of art.

οὖντες, ὅτι τὸ ἔνδον κινεῖ· ὥσπερ ἂν εἴ τις τὸ εἴδωλον
αὐτοῦ βλέπων ἀγνοῶν ὅθεν ἥκει ἐκεῖνο διώκοι. Δηλοῖ δέ,   35
ὅτι τὸ διωκόμενον ἄλλο καὶ οὐκ ἐν μεγέθει τὸ κάλλος, καὶ
τὸ ἐν τοῖς μαθήμασι κάλλος καὶ τὸ ἐν τοῖς ἐπιτηδεύμασι
καὶ ὅλως τὸ ἐν ταῖς ψυχαῖς· οὗ δὴ καὶ ἀληθείᾳ μᾶλλον
κάλλος, ὅταν τῳ φρόνησιν ἐνίδῃς καὶ ἀγασθῇς οὐκ εἰς τὸ
πρόσωπον ἀφορῶν—εἴη γὰρ ἂν τοῦτο αἶσχος—ἀλλὰ   40
πᾶσαν μορφὴν ἀφεὶς διώκῃς τὸ εἴσω κάλλος αὐτοῦ. Εἰ δὲ
μήπω σε κινεῖ, ὡς καλὸν εἰπεῖν τὸν τοιοῦτον, οὐδὲ σαυτὸν
εἰς τὸ εἴσω βλέψας ἡσθήσῃ ὡς καλῷ. Ὥστε μάτην ἂν οὕτως
ἔχων ζητοῖς ἐκεῖνο· αἰσχρῷ γὰρ καὶ οὐ καθαρῷ ζητήσεις·
Διὸ οὐδὲ πρὸς πάντας οἱ περὶ τῶν τοιούτων λόγοι· εἰ δὲ   45
καὶ σὺ εἶδες σαυτὸν καλόν, ἀναμνήσθητι.

2,34–35. εἴδωλον αὐτοῦ βλέπων. See the example of Narcissus in 1.6.8,8–12.

2,39. του = τινι, "in someone."

2,41. τὸ εἴσω κάλλος αὐτοῦ. For example, Socrates, who is visually ugly but beautiful within (see Alcibiades's speech in Plato, *Symp.* 215b–c).

2,41–46. See 1.6.9,29–30 for the idea that like is perceived by like, that one must make oneself beautiful to see both beauty outside and true beauty.

2,43. ἡσθήσει (sc. σεαυτῷ) ὡς καλῷ.

2,46. ἀναμνήσθητι. Supply τοὺς λόγους as object. A prerequisite for all philosophical endeavor is a morally ordered life. The Neoplatonists promoted this requirement by introductions to philosophy, commentaries on the *Ethics* of Aristotle or the treatises of Epictetus, and, not least, by works such as the lives of Pythagoras, which presented a model for the philosophical life of virtue. Before proceeding to apply ourselves to more complex metaphysical analysis (the λόγοι referred to in this passage), we are encouraged to purify our inner selves in order to make our intellects receptive. See 1.6.9. for these necessary preliminary preparations and 5.1.1–2 for the self-purification that begins with a turning away from externals and a realization of the nature and worth of the soul. It is at the same time a spiritual, moral, and intellectual exercise.

Bibliography

Primary Sources

Alexander of Aphrodisias

Caston, Victor, trans. 2012. *Alexander of Aphrodisias on the Soul: Part I,* London: Bristol Classical Press.
Sharples, Robert W., ed. 2008. *Alexander Aphrodisiensis De anima libri mantissa.* Berlin: De Gruyter.

Aristotle

Bywater, Ingram, ed. 1894. *Ethica Nicomachea.* Oxford: Clarendon.
Forster, Edward S., ed. and trans. 1989. *Posterior analytics; Topica.* LCL. London: Heinemann.
Ross, William D., trans. *Metaphysics.* 1924. Oxford: Clarendon.
———, trans. 1925. *Nicomachean Ethics.* Oxford: Clarendon.
———, ed. 1956. *De anima.* Oxford: Clarendon.
———, ed. 1957. *Metaphysica.* Oxford: Clarendon.
Smith, J. A., trans. 1984. *On the Soul.* In *The Complete Works of Aristotle in English.* Revised by Jonathan Barnes. 1984. Princeton: Princeton University Press.

Augustine

Dombart, Bernard, and Alphonse Kalb, eds. 1981. *De civitate dei.* Leipzig: Teubner.
Bettenson, Henry, trans. 1972. *Concerning the City of God against the Pagans.* Harmondsworth: Penguin.

Cicero

Hubbel, Harry M., ed. and trans. 1939. *Orator*. LCL. London: Heinemann.
King, John E., ed. and trans. 1966. *Tusculan Disputations*. LCL. London: Heinemann.

Dio of Prusa

Cohoon, James W., ed. and trans. 1939. *Discourses 12–30*. LCL. London: Heinemann.

Euripides

Nauck, J. August, ed. 1854. *Euripidis Tragoediae superstites et deperditarum fragmenta*. BSGRT. Leipzig: Teubner.

Heraclitus

Freeman, Kathleen, trans. 1971. *Ancilla to the Pre-Socratic Philosophers: A Complete Translation of the Fragments in Diels Fragmente der Vorsokratiker*. Oxford: Basil Blackwell.

Hierocles

Mullach, Friedrich W. A., ed. 1971. *In aureum pythagoreorum carmen commentarius*. Berlin: Geelhaar, 1853. Repr., Hildesheim: Gerstenberg.

Homer

Allen, Thomas W., ed. 1922. *Odyssey*. Oxford: Clarendon.
Munro, David B., and Thomas W. Allen, eds. 1920. *Iliad*. Oxford: Clarendon.

Origen

Chadwick, Henry, ed. and trans. 1965. *Contra Celsum*. Cambridge: Cambridge University Press.

Ovid

Miller, Frank J., ed. and trans. 1916. *Metamorphoses*. LCL. London: Heinemann.

Pausanias

Jones, William H. S., ed. and trans. 1935. *Description of Greece*. 5 vols. LCL. London: Heinemann.

Philostratus

Fairbank, Arthur, ed. and trans. 1931. *Imagines*. LCL. London: Heinemann.

Plato

Burnet, John, ed. 1900–1907. *Platonis opera*. 5 vols. Oxford: Oxford University Press.
Hamilton, Edith, and Huntington Cairns, eds. 1961. *The Collected Dialogues, Including the Letters*. New York: Pantheon.
Hackforth, Reginald. 1958. *Plato's Examination of Pleasure: A Translation of the Philebus*. Cambridge: Cambridge University Press.

Plotinus

Armstrong, Arthur Hilary. 1966–1982. *Plotinus, Enneads*. 7 vols. Loeb. Cambridge: Harvard University Press. Greek text with English translation and introductions.
Bréhier, Émile. 1924–1938. *Plotin, Ennéades*. 7 vols. Paris: Belles Lettres. Greek text and French translation with introductions and notes.
Brisson, Luc, and Jean François Pradeau, eds. 2002–2010. *Plotin Traités*. 8 vols. Paris: Flammarion. French translation and introductions.
Cilento, Vincenzo. 1947–1949. *Plotino, Enneadi*. 3 vols. Bari: Laterza. Italian translation and commentary.
Creuzer, Georg Friedrich. 1835. *Plotini Enneades*. Oxford: Oxford University Press. Greek text, with Marsilio Ficino's Latin translation and commentary.

Flamond, J.-M. *Ennead* 50 in *Traités 45–50*. Edited by Luc Brisson and J.-F. Pradeau. Paris: Flammarion, 2009.

Fleet, Barrie, trans. 2016. *Ennead IV.7: On the Immortality of the Soul*. Las Vegas: Parmenides.

Harder, Richard, Robert Beutler, and Willy Theiler. 1956–1971. *Plotins Schriften*. 12 vols. Hamburg: Meiner. Greek text with German translation and commentary.

Henry, Paul, and Hans-Rudolph Schwyzer. 1951–1973. *Plotini Opera*. Editio maior. 3 vols. Paris: Desclée De Brouwer; Brussels: L'Édition universelle. HS_1.

———. 1964–1982. *Plotini Opera*. Editio minor, with revised text. Oxford: Clarendon. HS_2.

———. 1973. "Addenda et Corrigenda ad textum et apparatum lectionum." In vol 3 of Henry and Schwyzer 1951–1973. HS_3.

———. 1982. "Addenda et Corrigenda ad textum et apparatum lectionum." In vol. 3 of Henry and Schwyzer 1964–1982. HS_4.

———. 1987. "Corrigenda ad Plotini Textum." *Museum Helveticum* 44:191–210. HS_5.

Igal, Jesus. 1982–1998. *Plotino, Enéadas*. 3 vols. Madrid: Gredos. Introduction, translations, and notes.

Kalligas, Paulos. 2006. *Plotinus Ennead I*. Athens: Akademia Athinon. Modern Greek.

Laurent, Jérôme. 2002. *Ennead 1* in *Traités 1–6*. Edited by Luc Brisson and Jean-François Pradeau. Paris: Flammarion.

MacKenna, Stephen. 1962. *Plotinus: The Enneads*. 3rd ed. London: Faber & Faber. English translation revised by B. S. Page.

———. 1991. *Plotinus. The Enneads*. London: Penguin. Selected treatises revised with notes by John Dillon.

Schwyzer, Hans-Rudolph. 1987. "Corrigenda ad Plotini Textum." *Museum Helveticum* 44:181–210. HS_5.

Porphyry

Armstrong, Arthur H., ed. and trans. 1969. *Porphyry on the Life of Plotinus and the Order of His Books; Ennead 1*. LCL. Cambridge: Harvard University Press.

Des Places, Édouard, ed. and trans. 1882. *Lettre à Marcella*. Paris: Belles Lettres.

Dillon, John M., trans. 2005. Pathways to the Intelligible." Pages 795–835 in volume 2 of *Porphyre Sentences*. Edited by Luc Brisson. Histoire des Doctrines de l'Antiquité Classique 33. Paris: Vrin.

Lamberz, Erich, ed. 1975. *Sententiae ad intelligibilia ducentes*. BSGRT. Leipzig: Teubner.

Smith, Andrew.1993. *Porphyrii Philosophi Fragmenta*. BSGRT. Stuttgart: Teubner.

Proclus

Dodds, Eric R., ed. and trans. 1963. *Elements of Theology*. 2nd ed. Oxford: Oxford University Press.

Secondary Sources

Anton, John P. 1964. "Plotinus' Refutation of Beauty as Symmetry." *JAAC* 23:233–37.

Armstrong, Arthur H. 1961. "Platonic *Eros* and Christian *Agape*." *Downside Review* 79:105–21. Repr. in *Plotinian and Christian Studies*. London: Variorum 1979.

———. 1974. "Tradition, Reason, and Experience in the Thought of Plotinus." Pages 171–94 in *Atti del convegno internazionale sul tema: Plotino e il neoplatonismo in Oriente e in Occidente (Roma, 5–9 Ottobre 1970)*. Rome: Accademia Nazionale dei Lincei.

Beierwaltes, Werner. 1961. "Die Metaphysik des Lichtes in der Philosophie des Plotins." *Zeitschrift für philosophische Forschung* 15:334–62.

Beierwaltes, Werner. 1980. Marsilio Ficinos Theorie des Schönen im Kontext des Platonismus. Sitzungsberichte der Heidelberger Akademie der Wissenschaften, Philosophisch-historische Klasse 11. Heidelberg: Winter.

Blumenthal, H. J. 1971. *Plotinus' Psychology: His Doctrines of the Embodied Soul*. The Hague: Nijhoff.

———. 1972. "Plotinus' Psychology: Aristotle in the Service of Platonism." *International Philosophical Quarterly* 12:340–64.

Emilsson, Eyjolfur Kjalar. 1988. *Plotinus on Sense-Perception: A Philosophical Study*. Cambridge: Cambridge University Press.

Hadot, Pierre. 1957. "Etre, Vie, Pensée chez Plotin et avant Plotin." Pages 105–41 In *Les sources de Plotin: Dix exposés et discussions*. Vendoeuvres: Fondation Hardt.

———. 1976. *Le mythe de Narcisse et son interpretation par Plotin*. Paris: Gallimard. Repr. as pages 225–66 in Hadot *Plotin, Porphyre: Études néoplatoniciennes*. Paris: Belles Lettres, 1999.

Lamberton, Robert. 1989. *Homer the Theologian: Neoplatonist Allegorical Reading and the Growth of the Epic Tradition*. Berkeley: University of California Press.

Long, Anthony A., and David N. Sedley. 1987. *The Hellenistic Philosophers*. 2 vols. Cambridge: Cambridge University Press.

Rist, J. M. 1967. *Plotinus: The Road to Reality*. Cambridge: Cambridge University Press.

Sedley, David 1997. " 'Becoming Like God' in the *Timaeus* and Aristotle." Pages 327–39 in *Interpreting the Timaeus-Critias*. Edited by Tomás Calvo and Luc Brisson. Sankt Augustin: Academia Verlag.

———. 1999. "The Idea of Godlikeness." Pages 309–28 in vol. 2 of *Plato*. Edited by Gail Fines. Oxford Readings in Philosophy. Oxford: Oxford University Press.

Smith, Andrew. 1974. *Porphyry's Place in the Neoplatonic Tradition*. The Hague: Nijhoff.

———. 1992. "Reason and Experience in Plotinus." Pages 21–30 in *At the Heart of the Real: Philosophical Essays in Honour of the Most Reverend Desmond Connell, Archbishop of Dublin*. Edited by Fran O'Rourke. Dublin: Irish Academic Press. Repr. as part VI in Smith, *Plotinus, Porphyry and Iamblichus: Philosophy and Religion in Neoplatonism*. London: Variorum, 2011.

———. 2011. "Image and Analogy in Plotinus." *Proceedings of the Boston Area Colloquium in Ancient Philosophy* 27:1–27.

———. 2014. "The Beauty of Divine Intellect in Plotinus." Pages 119–27 in *The Beauty of God's Presence in the Fathers of the Church*. Edited by Janet Elaine Rutherford. Dublin: Four Courts Press.

———. 2016. "Plotinus." Pages 772–74 in vol. 4 of *Augustinus-Lexicon*. Edited by Cornelius Mayer. Basel: Swabe.

Stamatellos, Giannis 2007. *Plotinus and the Presocratics*. Albany: State University of New York Press.

Wind, Edgar. 1968. *Pagan Mysteries in the Renaissance*. London.

CPSIA information can be obtained
at www.ICGtesting.com
Printed in the USA
FFHW020729101019
55480792-61271FF

PERIMETER

Joe Ballen, Book Two

David M. Kelly

Nemesis Press

PERIMETER : Joe Ballen, Book Two

Copyright ©2018 by David M. Kelly

All rights reserved. No part of this book may be reproduced in any form by any electronic or mechanical means including photocopying, recording, or information storage and retrieval without permission in writing from the author.

This is a work of fiction. Names, characters, places, and incidents either are the product of the author's imagination or are used fictitiously, and any resemblance to actual persons, living or dead, events, or locales is entirely coincidental.

ISBN-13: 978-0-9953294-8-5

ISBN-10: 0-9953294-8-6

First Published 2018

Nemesis Press
Wahnapitae, Ontario

www.nemesispress.com

Printed in U.S.A

Dedication

To my mother. Thank you for the dreams and the insanity, without which none of this would have happened.